MW00713991

PRAISE GOD
Common Prayer at Taizé

PRAISE GOD
Common Prayer at Taizé

New York
OXFORD UNIVERSITY PRESS
1977

First published in English in 1975

Published in French: "La Louange des Jours"
© France 1971 Les Presses de Taizé

Translated by Emily Chisholm
© France 1975 Les Presses de Taizé

First published in the United States of America 1977 by
Oxford University Press
200 Madison Avenue
New York, N.Y. 10016
Library of Congress Catalogue Card Number: 76-47437

Printed in the United States of America

Contents

As indicated in the Introduction, this volume does not include lists of readings, collects for each week, or a Psalter.

INTRODUCTION

'Common prayer' is almost too consecrated an expression in English, and we might forget that prayer 'in common' is a fundamental aspect of the life of the whole People of God. In the Acts of the Apostles, we read how the first Christian community in Jerusalem met together every day for prayer as one expression of a total community of life. But the roots of Christian common prayer go back into the prayer of the People of Israel. Prayer as a People, prayer as a whole community, prayer as a microcosm of the Church universal: common prayer is a different exercise to the more-or-less silent waiting on God 'in our rooms with the door shut' which we are inclined to consider as the main form of praying.

Today, there is a strong tendency to seek the freshness of new expressions, of spontaneity and of a sense of close community when Christians worship together. And there is also an urgent search for the strong bases on which a life of faith, love and service can grow. This tension between the spontaneous and the deeply-rooted, the new and the ancient, is a healthy one, so long as one is not sacrificed in favour of the other. The sources of prayer, as of faith, are to be found in the experience of the entire Church throughout the ages. The more resolutely we search, the more we see that the confrontation between our own immediate expressions and those coming from the roots of Christian living is necessary.

At Taizé, the search for the visible unity between Christians has always been integrated in a life of prayer and community. Over the years, the Community has evolved a form of common prayer which is still only a provisional one. The search for what is most rewarding in the traditions of common prayer found throughout the universal Church has always been one aspect of a more general search for a living community not cut off from the world of the late twentieth century. The universality of the Church, and its catholicity from the earliest

7

days, on the one hand, and concern to be present where the future of mankind is taking shape amongst the poorest of today's world: such have been the two poles of the life of the Community at Taizé from the start. Living 'a parable of Community', the Community has ever sought to celebrate a form of common prayer which would be at the same time firmly rooted in the great tradition of the Church's worship, but so adapted to our present-day mentalities that it would truly nourish and stimulate a daily commitment of love and service in the world today. Common prayer is always a 'sign of the eternity of God, of heaven on earth', but few today would care to see a liturgy which left untouched the great concerns common to Christians and to many others.

In addition, the ecumenical nature of the Community and its worship explain a deliberate attempt to draw on many different sources for this form of common prayer. There is an on-going search, so that the forms used at Taizé are always being revised. On the one hand, the changes of mentality amongst today's Christians are bound to stimulate the wish never to use language which is incomprehensible or needlessly specialised; on the other, the Church at large is hard at work and the forms used at Taizé change as the Church produces the results of new work.

Worship

"The Lord could do without our intercession and our praise. Yet it is the mystery of God that he should require us, his co-workers, to keep on praying and never lose heart." (The Rule of Taizé.) Prayer for the Christian is at the same time the prime necessity and something quite devoid of utility: to worship God and to express the fact that our communion with him is social as our humanity itself is social, but knowing that the Father gives us all we need before we even ask. The worship expressed by the People of God is offered in the name of the whole creation to the only Creator, in the assurance that in so doing, it is anticipating the aim for which all exists—the praise and glory of the eternal Father.

By his coming, his incarnation, death, resurrection and ascension, Christ opens wider perspectives—of Son-ship and Priesthood. The Church's worship is its participation in the sacrifice of submission and love made perfect on Calvary and offered eternally in the heavenly places. The communion of saints, the mystical Body of Christ, the Church in all its catholicity, prays in and with Christ before the throne and presence of the Father, set free of fear and sin by the victory of Christ. The liturgy of earth and the liturgy of heaven cannot be divided: the liturgy of faith, and the liturgy of Christ are the place of hope and communion for all mankind now and until the end of time.

The Holy Spirit is our participation in the mystery of God, by him we are made sons, and our prayer receives its sanctification in our hearts. He comes to help us, since we have no idea of how we ought to pray. He intercedes for us, and the flow of his intercession is a burning fire set by Christ on the earth, to burn until all is made new in the Kingdom of God.

Time

Our life is marked by a rhythm of darkness and light, of day and night, sleep and waking. These themes are also part of the Gospels, where they are a language of warfare. On the one hand we are offered the peaceful alternation of day and night, work then rest. But on the other, the constant challenge to 'stay awake and pray' with Christ in Gethsemane; we are set before the possibility of preferring darkness and death to the light of Christ. The People of God has always attached special importance to the moments in which this is apparent: sunset, dawn, midday. And with Christ the Church sees in those times the burial, the resurrection and the glory of the Son of God. In its liturgy, the Church remembers that for the Bible each day is present as soon as the sun has set, that the night which belongs to each day precedes it, preparing our strength in sleep. There is in that a sign of the optimism of faith, of impatience to run towards the Day which God offers.

In each week, Sunday is the first day, the day of Resurrection. For most Christians it is the day of common celebration of Christ in his Body the Church and in the Eucharist. How else shall we be able to celebrate him all through the week in our neighbour? Friday is marked by the memory of the dying of Jesus, and Saturday is the Sabbath when God rested in Christ in the deep silence of the tomb.

Christians celebrate the events of the life of Christ in a familiar yearly cycle. The *festival of the Incarnation* begins with Advent (a preparation for the coming of Christ), and stretches from Christmas (the Birth) to Epiphany (the Manifestation). The *festival of our Redemption* begins with Lent (a preparation for the obedience of Christ), passes through Holy Week in communion with the suffering and death of Christ before bursting out in the joy of Easter leading up to the fulfilment of Pentecost. The last Sunday of each festival is a celebration of the three persons of Godhead: after Epiphany in the Baptism of Christ, after Pentecost in Trinity Sunday. Between these great festivals run the *ordinary days* which cover the rest of the year.

From time to time the rhythm is broken by the celebration of one of the saints who have borne witness to Christ. The memorial of many is made simply during the Eucharist, but the great witnesses of the New Testament have so central a role that the joy of the Church expresses itself through a more complete liturgy of praise. Because within the great cloud of witnesses who from the earliest days have served Christ faithfully and humbly, certain names stand out: the Virgin Mary, John the Baptist, the Apostles and Evangelists, Stephen the first of the martyrs, on November 1st memorial is made of all the Communion of saints. The saints remind us that there are no privileges in the People of God, we are all of us called to be the saints of God. Each time that we gather in Christ's name, we live something of the joy of the saints at rest. All of us together wait on the coming of our Lord Jesus Christ, sanctified by the Spirit of love and forgiveness. All are caught up in the intercession offered by Christ before the throne of the Father. In our life day by day we recall that what has made the church so glad in the saints we

10

celebrate, is the fact of their faithfulness. There is in them a complete harmony beween faith and life: they were visibly bearers of Christ for those around them, including their persecutors. In the life of the saints we see the realisation of St John's question: If a person does not love his brother, whom he can see, how can he love God, whom he cannot see? The saints show us that in very simple ways this unity of love is also possible for us.

Contents

The People of God is the People of the Word. The constant fact that God has made himself known to worshipping mankind is the main reason for loving the expressions we receive from the great tradition of that worship. It would be hard to believe that today any one group of believers has so clear a vision of the glory of God that it could invent its liturgy without reference to the Word made known throughout the ages. In addition, we can say that as the People of God celebrates its Lord in the Word received, that Word penetrates the hearts of all who try to enter more deeply into it, and creates within them the spirit of worship. This cannot happen when worship becomes mechanical; neither can it happen when liturgy is reduced to elements which offer no difficulties to anybody.

So, the liturgy is called to be biblical. This it is by the use of *Psalms*, since that is the book of public worship for the People of God. Not all the Psalms are of equal value; they come to us in Christ, and certain of them seem to have little to do with the love of God made known in Jesus. In addition, *readings* from the Old and New Testaments have a central role in the liturgy. These readings, and indeed the whole of common prayer, do not dispense the individual from personal reading and prayer. But they serve to remind us that all Holy Scripture is the Book of a faithful People; the revelation of God is not to be separated from the celebration of that revelation together. Other elements have always figured in Christian worship. *Hymns*, or *songs*, compose a general response to the Word received. And by *prayers* it becomes possible to mark the liturgy with the realities of the present day.

In the Taizé liturgy, these elements are used as follows:

Psalms   : *Introduction — Psalm*;

Reading : *Old Testament — Gospel — Epistle — Short Reading*

Song   : *Responses — Hymn*

Prayer   : *Intercession — Collects — Free Prayer — Blessing*

On the present edition

A form of common prayer, however rich and meaningful, is not an end in itself. The end is the glory of God, in worship and life. The liturgy should stimulate lives of love and thankfulness, and our lives should bring us constantly to the worship and praise of God, in intercession for all mankind.

With this translation, it is hoped to make available in English of the present day a certain number of elements which may be of service where people are searching how to praise God together. At Taizé, in the context of a community of gifts, the working out of the liturgy has always been verbal and musical at the same time. For the liturgy of the People of God is a celebration in which music plays a major part. On the whole, the style of music best adapted for singing in French is not especially helpful when applied to English. For this reason, the words of the present edition are offered without music. In many places, there already exists a form of singing the Psalms, for example. This needs no adaptation. Others may wish to use a version of the Psalter in harmony with the rest of the forms: they will use the New Translation of the Psalms published by the Grail in Fontana Books (Collins, England). Music for the French Responses has been published: Répons de l'Office de Taizé (Desclée; Tournai, Belgium).

No set list of readings is included in this edition. It is felt that many such lists exist, and since what is best may vary according to circumstances, it would not be helpful to propose one. In those traditions where two readings are provided for morning and evening, a second reading can be included in the evening prayer.

After the first half of each office, 'Silence' is marked. This corresponds to the practice at Taizé. But in other places it may be felt useful to begin this silence with a short meditation or sermon. In small gatherings, a sharing around the texts read may be indicated. This silence, like the silence before the office begins and at the end, is part of the prayer together: our words are poor, and by simply being together we express the contemplative waiting of God's People. It is a moment when particular talents can be integrated into worship—music, for example.

After the silence in the evening, a hymn is indicated. This is another point in which traditions vary, and often it may be found that other hymns or more modern songs can be included. They ought not to be so numerous as to obscure the structure of the whole service. Often today, common prayer gains by being short.

The litany-form is used for the Intercession, either with a single response after each request, or in the form of a dialogue of versicles and responses. These can be sung or said, or at least the general response can be sung.

The collect for each week is to be found in the eucharistic liturgies of the various Churches, and is not included in this book. The General Collect should be given as the conclusion of the Free Prayer, summing up the various specific requests in terms of the liturgical season being celebrated. The Free Prayer will be very different according to circumstances, always having the intention of bringing together before God the concerns of each day.

*

The Taizé liturgy is not the official liturgy of a given Church, but is offered as the contribution of a Community to the research of the Church in many places. It is marked by a concern for clarity and universality. It may be that certain expressions are not always obvious. No Christian who is capable of it can neglect the need to study the sources of the Faith, especially in order to be able to read the Scriptures with understanding. The liturgy invites us to widen, not only our hearts, but also our intelligence; many riches only give up their secret slowly.

Psalms:

The following seem to be the psalms best adapted for the celebration of public worship, although the list is not rigorous. Certain verses of some of these psalms may be hard to understand. The numbering is that of the liturgical usage, as employed in the Fontana edition of the Gelineau Psalms.

1 2 3 4 5 6 8 9 10 12 14 15 17 18 19 21 22 23 24 25 26 28 29 30 31 32 33 37 38 39 40 41 42 45 46 47 50 54 55 56 60 61 62 64 65 66 67 68 69 70 71 76 79 80 81 83 84 85 87 88 89 90 92 94 95 96 97 98 99 101 102 103 106 110 111 112 113 114 115 117 118 (=11 groups of 2 sub-sections) 120 121 122 123 125 126 127 129 130 131 135 137 138 139 141 142 143 144 145 146 147 148 149 150.

Certain psalms are used in the Introductions, either in the ordinary days or the other liturgical periods. It is best not to use in the course of psalms those which already figure frequently in the liturgy by way of the introductions.

It is normal to conclude the psalms with the 'Glory be to the Father . . .' according to the usual forms.

The Antiphon to a Psalm is normally a line or two chosen from the text of the psalm, and used as a refrain before beginning the psalm, then at the end before and after the 'Glory be . . .'. The line should be chosen for its value as a summary of the love of God. At certain periods there are Antiphons set to mark the themes of the celebrations.

PRAISE GOD
Common Prayer at Taizé

Advent

In the time before Christmas, Advent is a period of preparation, as we repent and wait in hope for the coming Return of Christ.

God prepared for the *incarnation* of Christ within his People; the prophets, especially Isaiah, had announced him; then came John the Baptist to prepare for his coming. Advent reminds us that many were called to live in poverty as a sign that they were waiting for God to fulfil his promises; we know the names of certain witnesses whose waiting was humble and joyful: Mary and Joseph, Elizabeth and Zechariah, Anna and Simeon . . .

Advent is a time of waiting in *contemplation* for the presence of Christ within us; we are called to bear Christ, to live Christ for others. We too are invited to live that same spirit of poverty, of humility and joy.

15

SATURDAY EVENING

Introduction

Almighty Lord, come and revive us,
— Shine upon us and we shall be saved.

Your kindness, Lord, is over the land,
— You make the captives of Jacob return;
You take away the guilt of your People,
— You cover all their faults;
You withdraw your great anger,
— You return from the heat of your rage.

Praise to Him who is coming: the King, in the name of the Lord!
— Peace in heaven and glory in the highest! Amen.

Psalm — Epistle

Responses

O Lord, make us see your love!
— O Lord . . .

Grant us your salvation,
— Your love!

Glory to the Father, and the Son and the Holy Spirit.
— O Lord, make us see your love!

Silence — Hymn

Intercession

Heaven, shed your dew; Clouds, rain down salvation;
— Earth, bring forth the Saviour.

O Wisdom, from the mouth of the Most High! You reign over all things to the ends of the earth; come and teach us the way of wisdom.
— Lord Jesus, come soon!

16

O Lord, and Head of the house of Israel; you appeared to
Moses in the fire of the burning bush and you gave him the
law on Sinai; come with outstretched arm and ransom us.
— Lord Jesus, come soon!

O Branch of Jesse, standing as a sign among the nations;
before you kings will keep silence, and peoples will summon
you to their aid; come, set us free and delay no more.
— Lord Jesus, come soon!

O Key of David, and Sceptre of the House of Israel; you open
and none can shut, you shut and none can open; come, and
free the captive from prison.
— Lord Jesus, come soon!

O Morning Star, Splendour of the Light eternal and bright
Sun of Justice; come and enlighten all who live in darkness,
and in the shadow of death.
— Lord Jesus, come soon!

O King of the nations; you alone can fulfil their desires;
Cornerstone, you make opposing nations one; come and save
us. You formed us all from the clay.
— Lord Jesus, come soon!

O Emmanuel, Hope of the nations and their Saviour; come
and save us, Lord our God.
— Lord Jesus, come soon!

The Spirit and the Bride say, Come!
— Amen! Lord Jesus, come soon!

Collect for the week

The Lord be with you, — And also with you.
Let us pray to the Lord: *(silence, then the collect)* — Amen.

Free Prayer

General Collect

O Lord our God, may your grace increase in our hearts. Since we believe the incarnation of your beloved Son, bring us by his Passion and Cross to the glory of the Resurrection, for ever and ever,   — Amen.

Blessing

Holy, Holy, Holy, God the Lord!
— Sovereign Ruler of all the world.
He was, he is and he is coming.
— Yes, he is close at hand.

Let us bless the Lord.
— We give our thanks to God.

May God almighty bless us,
the Father, the Son and the Holy Spirit.
— Amen.

Introduction to the Gospel

(A Psalm or a hymn)
For the . . . Sunday in Advent, the Gospel according to . . .

Song of the Light

God has said: Let the light shine out of darkness!
— See, he has made his light shine in our hearts,
To shine with the light of the knowledge of his glory,
— In the face of Jesus Christ.
May God enlighten the sight of our hearts;
— And show us the hope in his call to us.
(or some other hymn)

SUNDAY MORNING

Introduction

Revive us now, God our Saviour,
— Restrain your resentment against us;
Will you keep your anger for ever?
— Your fury through all the ages?

For you are returning to revive us,
— And your People rejoices in you;
Lord, let us see your love,
— And grant us your salvation.

Psalm 79 (Shepherd of Israel . . .)

Short Reading

Brothers, the time has come to awaken from sleep, for salvation is closer now than when we first believed. The night is nearly over, the day is at hand; let us cast off the works of darkness and put on the armour of light.

Song of Zechariah

Antiphon for the 1st Sunday:
The Holy Spirit will come upon you,
the power of the Most High will overshadow you.

Antiphon for the 2nd Sunday:
Come, Lord, and visit us in peace.

Antiphon for the 3rd Sunday:
Heaven, shed your dew; Clouds, rain down salvation;
Earth, bring forth the Saviour.

Antiphon for the 4th Sunday:
Rejoice in the Lord; rejoice, for he is at hand.

Blessed be the Lord God of Israel,
coming to ransom his People;

Raising up saving power
in the house of his servant David,
as he said by the mouth of his prophets,
his saints in the times of old:

He sets us free from oppression,
free from the hands of our foes;
his bond of love with our fathers,
his covenant binding for ever;

His oath to our father Abraham,
assuring us, that liberated from fear,
delivered from all oppression,
we serve him in goodness and love,
before him, throughout our days.

You, child, to be called his prophet,
will walk in the presence of God,
to prepare the ways he shall come,
announcing his People's salvation
with pardon for all their sins.

Through the love in the heart of our God,
the rising Sun will come to us,
shining on those in the dark
who lie in the shadow of death,
and guiding our steps into peace.

Collect for the week

The Lord be with you — and also with you.
Let us pray to the Lord: *(silence, then the collect)* — Amen.

Introduction

Almighty Lord, come and revive us,
— Shine upon us and we shall be saved.

———

I am listening; what does God say?
— The word from God is peace,
Peace for his People and his friends,
— All who return in sincerity.
His salvation is near those who worship him,
— His Glory will live in our land.

———

Praise to Him who is coming: the King, in the name of the Lord!
— Peace in heaven and glory in the highest! Amen

Psalm — Epistle

Song of Mary

Antiphon for the 1st Sunday:
Here comes the Lord, he comes from far away,
the whole earth is full of his glory.

Antiphon for the 2nd Sunday:
The Virgin will conceive and give birth to a Son,
Emmanuel, God-with-us.

Antiphon for the 3rd Sunday:
Upon the throne of David, he will reign eternally, alleluia!

Antiphon for the 4th Sunday:
Jerusalem, burst into shouts of joy,
for your Saviour will come, alleluia!

My soul sings praises to the Lord,
my spirit glorifies my Saviour, my God!

For he has stooped to his humble servant,
and henceforth all ages will call me greatly blessed.
The Almighty chose me for his wonders;
Holy his Name!

And his love endures through the ages
to all who revere him;
he displays the strength of his arm,
and he scatters the conceited.

He will topple all the powerful from their thrones,
and raise up all the humble.
He feasts all the hungry with good cheer,
sends the rich away empty-handed.

He lifts up his own servant Israel,
ever remembering his love,
his ancient promise made to our fathers
in his oath to Abraham and to his race evermore.

Praise to Father, Son and Holy Spirit,
now and in the time to come,
and for ever and ever.

Silence — Hymn

Intercession

Heaven, shed your dew; Clouds, rain down salvation;
— Earth, bring forth the Saviour.

———

O Wisdom . . . *(as on Saturday evening)*

Collect for the week

The Lord be with you, — And also with you.
Let us pray to the Lord: *(silence, then the collect)* — Amen.

Free Prayer

22

General Collect

Receive, Lord God, the worship we raise as our evening offering; make us living torches for your Christ; since your grace delivers us from the works of darkness, may we hold firmly to your Word of life through Jesus Christ, your Son, our Lord,   — Amen

Blessing

Holy, Holy, Holy, God the Lord!
— Sovereign Ruler of all the world.
He was, he is and he is coming.
— Yes, he is close at hand.

Let us bless the Lord,
— We give our thanks to God.

May the Lord bless us, the Maker of heaven and earth.
— Amen.

MONDAY MORNING

Introduction

Almighty Lord, come and revive us,
— Shine upon us and we shall be saved.

_____

Truth and love have met,
— Justice and Peace have kissed;
Truth shall spring from the earth,
— And Justice look down from the heavens.

_____

Hosanna! Glory to Him who is coming in the name of the Lord!
— Blessed be the Kingdom that is coming! Amen

Psalm — Old Testament

Responses

To you, Lord, I lift up my soul.
 + My God, in you I hope.
— To you . . .

In you I hope all the day long,
Lord, for you are good.
— My God, in you I hope.

Remember your kindness, O Lord,
and your love, constant for ever.
— My God . . .

The secret of God is for all who fear him,
and his covenant, that they may know him.
— My God . . .

My eyes are fixed on the Lord,
for he draws my feet from the net.
— My God . . .

Glory to the Father, and the Son and the Holy Spirit.
— To you, Lord, I lift . . .

Gospel — Silence

Intercession

A voice crying in the desert: Prepare the way of the Lord!
— Make his paths level.

———

God the Father, you desired neither sacrifices nor offerings,
but you sent us your Beloved to reconcile all things in heaven
and on the earth through him, making peace by the blood of
his Cross:
— Glory to God who comes!

God the Son, Saviour of the world, you have shared our
humanity, you have been like us in all things but sin:
— Glory to God who comes!

God the Holy Spirit, you descended on Christ in whom lives
the fulness of godhead:
— Glory to God who comes!

O Christ, may your incarnation and your birth make us love
our human condition:
— Glory to God who comes!

May your perfect knowledge of the Scriptures strengthen us
in the Word of Life:
— Glory to God who comes!

May your faithfulness to your work make us each faithful in
our vocation:
— Glory to God who comes!

May your hidden life help us to live humbly:
— Glory to God who comes!

Collect for the week

The Lord be with you, — And also with you.
Let us pray to the Lord: *(silence, then the collect)* — Amen.

Free Prayer

General Collect

Lord God, our Father, by you we have been created and by
you we are led; in your goodness shed your light into our
hearts, that we may always live in you, through Jesus Christ
our Lord,   — Amen.

The Lord's Prayer

O Christ, remember us in your Kingdom:
— Lord, teach us to pray: Our Father . . .

Blessing

Let us bless the Lord,
— We give our thanks to God.

May the God of hope fill us with all joy and all peace in
believing, that we may be overflowing with hope through the
power of the Holy Spirit.   — Amen.

MONDAY EVENING

Introduction

Almighty Lord, come and revive us,
— Shine upon us and we shall be saved.

———

God himself gives us his joy,
— And our land yields its fruit;
Justice will walk before him,
— Peace comes in his footsteps.

———

Praise to Him who is coming: the King, in the name of the Lord!
— Peace in heaven and glory in the highest! Amen.

Psalm — Epistle

Responses

Almighty Lord, come and revive us!
— Almighty Lord . . .

Shine upon us and we shall be saved,
— Come and revive us!

Glory to the Father, and the Son and the Holy Spirit.
— Almighty Lord, come and revive us!

Silence — Hymn

Intercession

Heaven, shed your dew; Clouds, rain down salvation;
— Earth, bring forth the Saviour.

———

God Almighty, we bless you for calling us to know you, to love and to serve you in spite of all we do wrong.
— Maranatha, the Lord is coming!

27

You have sent your beloved Son, your perfect image and the reflection of your glory; for our salvation you have revealed him in our humanity, intending him to be like us in all things but sin.
— Maranatha, the Lord is coming!

In him you enlighten our ignorance by the light of the Gospel; you proclaim your Kingdom for us; you wash away our offences and you heal our infirmities.
— Maranatha, the Lord is coming!

O God, you love all your creatures; keep us in the grace of Christ and the ways of your goodness; may we peacefully await the day when he returns in his glory.
— Maranatha, the Lord is coming!

Grant us your peace; may we share it one with another in brotherly love and offer you our spiritual worship, consecrating our lives to your praise and to the service of our neighbours.
— Maranatha, the Lord is coming!

Collect for the week

The Lord be with you, — And also with you.
Let us pray to the Lord: *(silence, then the collect)* — Amen.

Free Prayer

General Collect

Lord, may we live simply, justly and devoutly as we await the appearing in glory of our God and Saviour Jesus Christ; he gave himself for us, and so set us apart as a People of his own, for he lives and reigns for ever,   — Amen.

Blessing

Holy, Holy, Holy, God the Lord!
— Sovereign Ruler of all the world.
He was, he is and he is coming.
— Yes, he is close at hand.

Let us bless the Lord,
— We give our thanks to God.

May the God of peace sanctify us wholly, keeping us blameless in body, mind and soul for the Coming of our Lord Jesus Christ.
— Amen.

Introduction

Almighty Lord, come and revive us,
— Shine upon us and we shall be saved.

———

Lord, you are returning to revive us,
— And your People rejoices in you;
Lord, let us see your love,
— And grant us your salvation.

———

Hosanna! Glory to Him who is coming in the name of the Lord!
— Blessed be the Kingdom that is coming! Amen.

Psalm — Old Testament

Responses

Lord, come down and save us all!
+ Almighty God, come and revive us!
— Lord, come down . . .

Shepherd of Israel hear us; throned above the Cherubim,
Shine down on us!
— Almighty God . . .

Rise up, O God, in your strength, and come to our rescue.
— Almighty God . . .

God of all, return and save,
look down from heaven and see!
— Almighty God . . .

Visit this vine and protect it;
for it has grown in your loving care.
— Almighty God . . .

Glory to the Father, and the Son, and the Holy Spirit.
— Lord, come down and save . . .

Gospel — Silence

Intercession

A voice crying in the desert: Prepare the way of the Lord!
— Make his paths level.

———

We give you thanks, O God, for revealing your power in the
creation of the universe, and for your providence in the life
of the world, for man made in your image to rule in your
name over the other creatures.
— We bless your holy Name!

For the victory of light over darkness, of truth over error, for
the knowledge of your prophetic word setting us free from
fear and despair, for the advancement of your reign of justice
and of peace, of holiness and of love.
— We bless your holy Name!

For the revelation of your Kingdom among us by your Son,
Jesus Christ, who came on earth to manifest and to accomplish your will; for his humble birth and his holy life, for his
words and miracles, for his sufferings and death, for his entry
into kingship by his resurrection and ascension.
— We bless your holy Name!

For the founding of the universal Church spread to the ends
of the earth, for the coming of your Kingdom within us by the
gifts of your Holy Spirit, and for the advent of your Kingdom
in the ends of time when you will be all in all.
— We bless your holy Name!

Collect for the week

The Lord be with you, — And also with you.
Let us pray to the Lord: *(silence, then the collect)* — Amen.

Free Prayer

General Collect

Lord, you have brought us out of the power of darkness into the Kingdom of your dear Son; may we wait for his coming in the knowledge that we are in the world but not of the world, since he reigns in your Eternity for ever and ever,   —Amen.

The Lord's Prayer

O Christ, remember us in your Kingdom:
— Lord, teach us to pray: Our Father . . .

Blessing

Let us bless the Lord.
— We give our thanks to God.

May the Lord bless us and keep us; may Christ smile upon us and give us his grace; may he unveil his face to us and bring us his peace.
— Amen.

TUESDAY EVENING

Introduction

Almighty Lord, come and revive us,
— Shine upon us and we shall be saved.

————

I am listening; what does God say?
— The word from God is peace,
Peace for his People and his friends,
— All who return in sincerity.
His salvation is near those who worship him,
— His Glory will live in our land.

————

Praise to Him who is coming: the King, in the name of the Lord!
— Peace in heaven and glory in the highest! Amen.

Psalm — Epistle

Responses

Arise, shine, for your light has come!
— Arise . . .

And the Glory of the Lord has risen upon you.
— Your light has come!

Glory to the Father, and the Son and the Holy Spirit.
— Arise, shine, for your light has come!

Silence — Hymn

Intercession

Heaven, shed your dew; Clouds, rain down salvation;
— Earth, bring forth the Saviour.

————

Lord, remember your Church; send her continually your Spirit of unity, courage and holiness.
— Always be with us, Lord Emmanuel.

33

By shedding your blood, you have purified your Church; keep us ready to welcome the Day of your coming.
— Always be with us, Lord Emmanuel.

Give to each one of us your Spirit of holiness and wisdom, in the fulfilling of the ministries to which you have called us; bring us to your presence.
— Always be with us, Lord Emmanuel.

We pray you for all who are leading the nations: give them a sense of what is right, that they may work towards peace and full life for all.
— Always be with us, Lord Emmanuel.

Call from amongst us bearers of your communion; may they go to the far ends of the earth as tokens of your friendship and signs of your light.
— Always be with us, Lord Emmanuel.

Give to all who believe and who seek you a Spirit of prayer and of thankfulness; so we shall give you thanks and bless you in all the days of our life.
— Always be with us, Lord Emmanuel.

Collect for the week

The Lord be with you, — And also with you.
Let us pray to the Lord: *(silence, then the collect)* — Amen.

Free Prayer

General Collect

O God, when the Angel came to greet Mary, it was your will that your only Son should take flesh: may such humility always be ours through Christ our Lord,   — Amen.

Blessing

Holy, Holy, Holy, God the Lord!
— Sovereign Ruler of all the world.
He was, he is and he is coming.
— Yes, he is close at hand.

Let us bless the Lord,
— We give our thanks to God.

May the Lord of peace give us peace in all ways and at all times.
— Amen.

Introduction to the Gospel

(On the Wednesday of the third week in Advent, Memorial of the Annunciation; the Gospel of the Annunciation is proclaimed on the Tuesday evening, as on a Saturday evening)

The Virgin will conceive, and bear a Son,
Emmanuel, God-with-us.
— The Virgin . . .

Blessed be the Lord God of Israel;
coming to ransom his People.
— The Virgin . . .

Gospel of the Annunciation of the Angel to Mary, according to Luke (Luke; I. 26-38).

Song of the Light
(as on Saturdays, or some other hymn.)

Introduction

Almighty Lord, come and revive us,
— Shine upon us and we shall be saved.

———

Truth and love have met,
— Justice and Peace have kissed;
Truth shall spring from the earth,
— And Justice look down from the heavens.

———

Hosanna! Glory to Him who is coming in the name of the Lord!
— Blessed be the Kingdom that is coming! Amen.

Psalm — Old Testament

Responses

My soul is waiting for the Lord,
+ I am sure of his Word.
— My soul is waiting...

From the depths I cry to you, Lord:
hear my prayer!
— I am sure of his Word!

Forgiveness is found with you:
I hope for you in awe.
— I am sure of his Word!

My soul longs more for the Lord
than a watchman for the dawn.
— I am sure of his Word!

Let the watchman count on the dawn,
and Israel on the Lord!
— I am sure of his Word!

Glory to the Father, and the Son and the Holy Spirit.
— My soul is waiting . . .

Gospel — Silence

Intercession

A voice crying in the desert: Prepare the way of the Lord!
— Make his paths level.

———

Let us stand alert and full of joy. Let us rejoice and implore
the Lord, saying: Kyrie eleison (*or*: Lord, have mercy).
— Kyrie eleison.

O God, in your measureless love you have fashioned humanity,
making us glorious by the image of your Glory; hear us, we
pray:
— Kyrie eleison.

Through Abraham you promised happiness to all who love
you, and by the manifestation of Christ you have made yourself known to your Church; hear us, we pray.
— Kyrie eleison.

When we wander in darkness, you do not leave us, but restore
us to the light of your forgiveness; hear us, we pray.
— Kyrie eleison.

Sanctify in love the whole body of your People, we pray.
— Kyrie eleison.

Lord, you govern all the worlds in your love; hear us, we pray.
— Kyrie eleison.

Give us the victory, Lord Jesus Christ, when you come; set
peace in your Church, and hear us, we pray.
— Kyrie eleison.

Collect for the week

The Lord be with you, — And also with you.
Let us pray to the Lord: *(silence, then the collect)* — Amen.

Free Prayer

General Collect

O God, you disperse our fears by the light of your Word; strengthen our hearts in faith, that the fire of love kindled in them by your Holy Spirit may never be stifled by temptation; give us this through Jesus Christ, our Lord,   — Amen.

The Lord's Prayer

O Christ, remember us in your Kingdom:
— Lord, teach us to pray: Our Father . . .

Blessing

Let us bless the Lord,
— We give our thanks to God.

May the God of patience and of consolation grant us to live together after the pattern of our Lord Jesus Christ, so that with one heart and one voice we may give glory to God, the Father of our Lord Jesus Christ.
— Amen.

WEDNESDAY EVENING

Introduction

Almighty Lord, come and revive us,
— Shine upon us and we shall be saved.

———

God himself gives us his joy
— And our land yields its fruit;
Justice will walk before him,
— Peace comes in his footsteps.

———

Praise to Him who is coming: the King, in the name of the Lord!
— Peace in heaven and glory in the highest! Amen.

Psalm — Epistle

Responses

O Lord, make us see your love!
— O Lord . . .

Grant us your salvation,
— Your love!

Glory to the Father, and the Son and the Holy Spirit.
— O Lord, make us see your love!

Silence—Hymn

Intercession

Heaven, shed your dew; Clouds, rain down salvation;
— Earth, bring forth the Saviour.

———

O Wisdom, from the mouth of the Most High; you reign over all things to the ends of the earth; come and teach us the way of wisdom.
— Lord Jesus, come soon!

39

O Lord, and Head of the house of Israel; you appeared to Moses in the fire of the burning bush and you gave him the law on Sinai; come with outstretched arm and ransom us.
— Lord Jesus, come soon!

O Branch of Jesse, standing as a sign among the nations; before you kings will keep silence, and peoples will summon you to their aid; come, set us free and delay no more.
— Lord Jesus, come soon!

O Key of David, and Sceptre of the House of Israel; you open and none can shut, you shut and none can open; come, and free the captive from prison.
— Lord Jesus, come soon!

O Morning Star, Splendour of the Light eternal and bright Sun of Justice; come and enlighten all who live in darkness, and in the shadow of death.
— Lord Jesus, come soon!

O King of the nations; you alone can fulfil their desires; Cornerstone, you make opposing nations one; come and save us. You formed us all from the clay.
— Lord Jesus, come soon!

O Emmanuel, Hope of the nations and their Saviour; come and save us, Lord our God.
— Lord Jesus, come soon!

The Spirit and the Bride say, Come!
— Amen! Lord Jesus, come soon!

Collect for the week

The Lord be with you, — And also with you.
Let us pray to the Lord: *(silence, then the collect)* — Amen.

Free Prayer

40

General Collect

O God, the voice of your prophets, and their whole lives, announced the coming of your salvation; may we in our turn faithfully live Christ for others, until that Day when we shall see him face to face as he comes to save us all; grant this through Jesus, your Christ, our Lord, — Amen.

Blessing

Holy, Holy, Holy, God the Lord!
— Sovereign Ruler of all the world.
He was, he is and he is coming.
— Yes, he is close at hand.

Let us bless the Lord,
— We give our thanks to God.

May our Lord Jesus Christ himself, and God our Father who has loved us, and given us by his grace eternal consolation and joyful hope, comfort our hearts and strengthen them in every good word and work.
— Amen.

THURSDAY MORNING

Introduction

Almighty Lord, come and revive us,
— Shine upon us and we shall be saved.

Lord, you are returning to revive us,
— And your People rejoices in you;
Lord, let us see your love,
— And grant us your salvation.

Hosanna! Glory to Him who is coming in the name of the Lord!
— Blessed be the Kingdom that is coming! Amen.

Psalm — Old Testament

Responses

To you, Lord, I lift up my soul.
+ My God, in you I hope.
— To you . . .

In you I hope all the day long,
Lord, for you are good.
— My God, in you I hope.

Remember your kindness, O Lord,
and your love, constant for ever.
— My God, in you I hope.

The secret of God is for all who fear him,
and his covenant, that they may know him.
— My God . . .

My eyes are fixed on the Lord,
for he draws my feet from the net.
— My God . . .

Glory to the Father, and the Son and the Holy Spirit.
— To you, Lord, I lift . . .

Gospel — Silence

Intercession

A voice crying in the desert: Prepare the way of the Lord!
— Make his paths level.

———

God the Father . . . *(as on Monday morning)*

Collect for the week

The Lord be with you, — And also with you.
Let us pray to the Lord: *(silence, then the collect)* — Amen.

Free Prayer

General Collect

O Christ, splendour of the glory of God and perfect image of
the Father; we give you thanks for the infinite love which sent
you among us; we confess you light and life of the world; and
we adore you as our Lord and our God, now and for ever,
— Amen.

The Lord's Prayer

O Christ, remember us in your Kingdom;
— Lord, teach us to pray: Our Father . . .

Blessing

Let us bless the Lord,
— We give our thanks to God.

May the God of peace enable us to do his will in every kind
of goodness, working in us what pleases him, through Jesus
Christ, to whom be the glory for ever and ever.
— Amen.

43

THURSDAY EVENING

Introduction

Almighty Lord, come and revive us,
— Shine upon us and we shall be saved.

———

I am listening; what does God say?
— The word from God is peace,
Peace for his People and his friends,
— All who return in sincerity.
His salvation is near those who worship him,
— His Glory will live in our land.

———

Praise to Him who is coming: the King, in the name of the Lord!
— Peace in heaven and glory in the highest! Amen.

Psalm — Epistle

Responses

Almighty Lord, come and revive us!
— Almighty Lord . . .

Shine upon us and we shall be saved,
— Come and revive us!

Glory to the Father, and the Son and the Holy Spirit.
— Almighty Lord, come and revive us!

Silence — Hymn

Intercession

Heaven, shed your dew; Clouds, rain down salvation;
— Earth, bring forth the Saviour.

———

God Almighty, we bless you for calling us to know you, to love and to serve you in spite of all we do wrong.
— Maranatha, the Lord is coming!

44

You have sent your beloved Son, your perfect image and the reflection of your glory; for our salvation you have revealed him in our humanity, intending him to be like us in all things but sin.
— Maranatha, the Lord is coming!

In him you enlighten our ignorance by the light of the Gospel; you proclaim your Kingdom for us; you wash away our offences and you heal our infirmities.
— Maranatha, the Lord is coming!

O God, you love all your creatures; keep us in the grace of Christ and the ways of your goodness; may we peacefully await the day when he returns in his glory.
— Maranatha, the Lord is coming!

Grant us your peace; may we share it one with another in brotherly love and offer you our spiritual worship, consecrating our lives to your praise and to the service of our neighbours.
— Maranatha, the Lord is coming!

Collect for the week

The Lord be with you, — And also with you.
Let us pray to the Lord: *(silence, then the collect)* — Amen.

Free Prayer

General Collect

God of light and glory; shine upon us in this evening darkness, making our hearts thankful for all your kindnesses, through Jesus Christ, your Son, our Lord,   — Amen.

Blessing

Holy, Holy, Holy, God the Lord!
— Sovereign Ruler of all the world.
He was, he is and he is coming.
— Yes, he is close at hand.

Let us bless the Lord,
— We give our thanks to God.

May the grace of our Lord Jesus Christ, the love of God and
the communion of the Holy Spirit be with us all.
— Amen.

Introduction to the Gospel

*(On the Friday of the third week in Advent, memorial of the
Visitation of Mary to Elizabeth; on the Thursday evening
the Gospel of the Visitation is proclaimed as on a Saturday.)*

Come Lord and visit us in peace.
– Come Lord . . . *(or another hymn)*

For the Visitation of Mary to Elizabeth, the Gospel according to Luke: (Luke; I. 39-46)

Song of Mary

My soul sings praises to the Lord,
my spirit glorifies my Saviour, my God!

For he has stooped to his humble servant,
and henceforth all ages will call me greatly blessed.
The Almighty chose me for his wonders;
Holy his Name!

And his love endures through the ages
to all who revere him;
he displays the strength of his arm,
and he scatters the conceited.

He will topple all the powerful from their thrones,
and raise up all the humble.
He feasts all the hungry with good cheer,
sends the rich away empty-handed.

He lifts up his own servant Israel,
ever remembering his love,
his ancient promise made to our fathers
in his oath to Abraham and to his race evermore.

Praise to Father, Son and Holy Spirit,
now and in the time to come
and for ever and ever.

FRIDAY MORNING

Introduction

Almighty Lord, come and revive us,
— Shine upon us and we shall be saved.

————

Truth and love have met,
— Justice and Peace have kissed;
Truth shall spring from the earth,
— And Justice look down from the heavens.

————

Hosanna! Glory to Him who is coming in the name of the Lord!
— Blessed be the Kingdom that is coming! Amen.

Psalm — Old Testament

Responses

Lord, come down and save us all!
+ Almighty God, come and revive us!
— Lord, come down . . .

Shepherd of Israel hear us; throned above the Cherubim,
Shine down on us!
— Almighty God . . .

Rise up, O God, in your strength, and come to our rescue.
— Almighty God . . .

God of all, return and save,
look down from heaven and see!
— Almighty God . . .

Visit this vine and protect it;
for it has grown in your loving care.
— Almighty God . . .

Glory to the Father, and the Son, and the Holy Spirit.
— Lord, come down and save . . .

Gospel — Silence

Intercession

A voice crying in the desert: Prepare the way of the Lord!
— Make his paths level.

———

We give you thanks, O God, for revealing your power in the creation of the universe, and for your providence in the life of the world, for man made in your image to rule in your name over the other creatures.
— We bless your holy Name!

For the victory of light over darkness, of truth over error, for the knowledge of your prophetic word setting us free from fear and despair, for the advancement of your reign of justice and of peace, of holiness and of love.
— We bless your holy Name!

For the revelation of your Kingdom among us by your Son, Jesus Christ, who came on earth to manifest and to accomplish your will; for his humble birth and his holy life, for his words and miracles, for his sufferings and death, for his entry into kingship by his resurrection and ascension.
— We bless your holy Name!

For the founding of the universal Church spread to the ends of the earth, for the coming of your Kingdom within us by the gifts of your Holy Spirit and for the advent of your Kingdom in the ends of time when you will be all in all.
— We bless your holy Name!

Collect for the week

The Lord be with you,—And also with you.
Let us pray to the Lord: *(silence, then the collect)* — Amen.

Free Prayer

49

General Collect

O God, confirm us in faith; may we recognize in the Virgin's Son our only Saviour, true God and true man; and by his resurrection bring us to freedom and eternal joy: for he lives and reigns with you and the Holy Spirit now and for ever,
— Amen.

The Lord's Prayer

O Christ, remember us in your Kingdom:
— Lord, teach us to pray: Our Father ...

Blessing

Let us bless the Lord,
— We give our thanks to God.

May God the Father, and our Lord Jesus Christ, grant us peace and love in believing.
— Amen.

FRIDAY EVENING

Introduction

Almighty Lord, come and revive us,
— Shine upon us and we shall be saved.

———

God himself gives us his joy
— And our land yields its fruit;
Justice will walk before him,
— Peace comes in his footsteps.

———

Praise to Him who is coming: the King, in the name of the Lord!
— Peace in heaven and glory in the highest! Amen.

Psalm — Epistle

Responses

Arise, shine, for your light has come!
— Arise . . .

And the Glory of the Lord has risen upon you.
— Your light has come!

Glory to the Father, and the Son and the Holy Spirit.
— Arise, shine, for your light has come!

Silence — Hymn

Intercession

Heaven, shed your dew; Clouds rain down salvation;
— Earth, bring forth the Saviour.

———

Give joy, Lord, to all your faithful servants; may they follow you all the days of their life.
— Always be with us, Lord Emmanuel.

Shed within us your Spirit of charity; may we never close our hearts to any of our brothers.
— Always be with us, Lord Emmanuel.

Give an end to the divisions between Christians; gather us in one visible communion.
— Always be with us, Lord Emmanuel.

Look upon all who suffer persecution for your name's sake; uphold them by your strong Spirit, that they may witness to you in all their trials.
— Always be with us, Lord Emmanuel.

Look upon all who are suffering in their hearts or their bodies; give them health and peace to sing your power.
— Always be with us, Lord Emmanuel.

Give eternal rest to all who are dying; may the light that never sets shine upon them.
— Always be with us, Lord Emmanuel.

Collect for the week

The Lord be with you, — And also with you.
Let us pray to the Lord: *(silence, then the collect)* — Amen.

Free Prayer

General Collect

O Christ, the only Son and eternal Word of the Father; on the Cross you gave your life for our sins. Accept this evening worship which we offer now, in communion with all who confess your name; you live and reign for ever and ever,
— Amen.

Blessing

Holy, Holy, Holy, God the Lord!
— Sovereign Ruler of all the world.
He was, he is and he is coming.
— Yes, he is close at hand.

Let us bless the Lord,
— We give our thanks to God.

May the God of all grace, who has called us to his eternal glory in Christ, after we have suffered for a while, make us perfect, confirm and strengthen us; to him be the power for ever and ever.
— Amen.

SATURDAY MORNING

Introduction

Almighty Lord, come and revive us,
— Shine upon us and we shall be saved.

———

Lord, you are returning to revive us,
— And your People rejoices in you;
Lord, let us see your love,
— And grant us your salvation.

———

Hosanna! Glory to Him who is coming in the name of the
Lord!
— Blessed be the Kingdom that is coming! Amen.

Psalm — Old Testament

Responses

My soul is waiting for the Lord,
  + I am sure of his Word.
— My soul is waiting . . .

From the depths I cry to you, Lord:
hear my prayer!
— I am sure of his Word!

Forgiveness is found with you:
I hope for you in awe.
— I am sure of his Word!

My soul longs more for the Lord
than a watchman for the dawn.
— I am sure of his Word!

Let the watchman count on the dawn,
and Israel on the Lord!
— I am sure of his Word!

Glory to the Father, and the Son and the Holy Spirit.
— My soul is waiting . . .

Gospel — Silence

Intercession

A voice crying in the desert: Prepare the way of the Lord!
— Make his paths level.

———

Let us stand alert and full of joy. Let us rejoice and implore
the Lord, saying: Kyrie eleison (*or*: Lord, have mercy)
— Kyrie eleison.

O God, in your measureless love you have fashioned humanity,
making it glorious by the image of your Glory; hear us, we
pray:
— Kyrie eleison.

Through Abraham you promised happiness to all who love
you, and by the manifestation of Christ you have made yourself known to your Church; hear us, we pray.
— Kyrie eleison.

When we wander in darkness, you do not leave us, but restore
us to the light of your forgiveness; hear us, we pray.
— Kyrie eleison.

Sanctify in love the whole body of your People, we pray.
— Kyrie eleison.

Lord, you govern all the world in your love; hear us, we pray.
— Kyrie eleison.

Give us the victory, Lord Jesus Christ, when you come; set
peace in your Church, and hear us, we pray.
— Kyrie eleison.

Collect for the week

The Lord be with you, — And also with you.
Let us pray to the Lord: *(silence, then the collect)* — Amen.

Free Prayer

General Collect

Almighty Father, you have sent into the world your only-begotten Son; may we so set our lives in him, that we be found with him in the eternity of his Kingdom, for he reigns for evermore,   — Amen.

The Lord's Prayer

O Christ, remember us in your Kingdom:
— Lord, teach us to pray: Our Father . . .

Blessing

Let us bless the Lord,
— We give our thanks to God.

May the peace of God, which surpasses all understanding, keep our hearts and our minds in Christ Jesus.
— Amen.

Christmas

Christmas is a period of festival, and not only one day. The Birth of Christ, celebrated in the night of December 25, is only one of the events by which the Church recognises, by faith, the presence of God with us.

At the other extremity of the Christmas season stands the Epiphany (Manifestation). In fact, the entire festival is a celebration of God's Appearing, and should be related to the Appearing of the Risen Christ after Easter.

In the poverty of his birth, as in the adoration of the shepherds, in the mysterious gifts of the Wise Men come from outside the People of the Old Alliance, always the Church directs our attention to the mystery of Christ. After the celebration of the Epiphany, come Sundays evoking Christ's Baptism and the first Sign at the Marriage-Feast of Cana. Always, the faith of the Church coming in response to the question: But who is this man?

A celebration of the humble hidden-ness of God with us in our poverty, and a proclamation no longer limited to one particular nation, but announced for all mankind, in every place and time.

FOR THE EVES OF THE FESTIVALS AND
SATURDAY EVENINGS

Introduction

Blessed be the Lord who alone has worked wonders!
— Blessed be his glorious Name for ever!

———

Let us come into the place of his Presence,
— Let us bow down at his footstool!
Rise, Lord, and come to your resting-place,
— Come with the ark of your strength!

———

Glory to God, glory in the highest, Alleluia!
— And peace on earth to all whom he loves, Alleluia!

Psalm — Epistle

Responses

The Word was made flesh, Alleluia, Alleluia!
— The Word . . .

He dwelt among us,
— Alleluia, Alleluia!

Glory to the Father, and the Son and the Holy Spirit.
— The Word was made flesh, Alleluia, Alleluia!

on January 5th, or the eve of Epiphany Sunday:
They come hurrying from far and wide, Alleluia, Alleluia!
— They come hurrying . . .

Bringing gold, and frankincense, and myrrh,
— Alleluia, Alleluia!

Glory to the Father, and the Son and the Holy Spirit.
— They come hurrying from far and wide, Alleluia, Alleluia!

Silence — Hymn

Intercession

All the ends of the earth have seen the salvation of our God, Alleluia!
— Acclaim the Lord, all the earth, Alleluia!

January 5:
We have seen his star in the East, Alleluia!
— And we have come to worship him, Alleluia!

———

Lord, have mercy!
— Christ, have mercy!

Lord, have mercy!
— Christ, hear us!

God, the Father of heaven,
— Mercy for us!

God the Son, Redeemer of the world,
— Mercy for us!

God, the Holy Spirit,
— Mercy for us!

God, one God, thrice holy,
— Mercy for us!

Jesus, Son of the living God, splendour of the Father, Light eternal, King of glory, Sun of justice, born of the Virgin Mary:
— Glory to you, O Lord!

Jesus, Wonderful Counsellor, strong Lord, eternal God, Prince of peace:
— Glory to you, O Lord!

Jesus, most powerful, patient, obedient, gentle and humble of heart, loving all who are pure in heart:
— Glory to you, O Lord!

Jesus, God of peace, Source of life, Pattern of holiness, friend of all, our God and our Refuge:
— Glory to you, O Lord!

Jesus, Brother of the poor, Treasure of the faithful, Good Shepherd, true Light, inexhaustible Wisdom, boundless love, our Way and our Life:
— Glory to you, O Lord!

Jesus, joy of the angels, king of the patriarchs, master of the Apostles, teacher of the Evangelists, strength of the martyrs, light of every witness to the truth, Crown of all the saints:
— Glory to you, O Lord!

Lamb of God, you take away the sin of the world:
— Lord, forgive!

Lamb of God, you take away the sin of the world:
— Lord, hear us!

Lamb of God, you take away the sin of the world:
— Lord, have mercy on us!

Collect for the day

The Lord be with you, — And also with you.
Let us pray to the Lord: *(silence, then the collect)* — Amen.

Free Prayer

General Collect

Eternal Lord, God of inaccessible light; you make yourself known to fulfil our every longing. May the desires of our hearts find in you their object, lead us into your Kingdom and sanctify your People in every kind of good, through Jesus Christ, our Lord,   — Amen.

Blessing

He was revealed in the flesh,
— Justified in the Spirit,
Contemplated by the angels,
— Proclaimed among the nations,
Believed in the world,
— Taken up into glory!

Let us bless the Lord.
— We give our thanks to God.

May God almighty bless us,
the Father, the Son and the Holy Spirit.
— Amen.
(Then may follow a reading of the next day's Gospel and the Song of Simeon)

Introduction

Lord, your priests are clothed in righteousness,
— Your faithful People sings for joy.
For the sake of David your servant
— Have pity and come to your People.

The Lord has sworn to David,
— His word will be true for ever:
A son of your body I will set
— To rule on the throne meant for you.

Psalm

For Christmas, its Octave and Epiphany: Psalm 97
For the Baptism of Christ (1st Sunday after 6 January): Psalm 28

Short Reading

God, who in former days, so many times and in so many ways, had spoken to our fathers by the prophets, has spoken to us in these last days by his Son, whom he has established heir of all things and by whom he made the worlds.

Song of Zechariah

Antiphon of the Nativity:
Now the prophecies are fulfilled:
the light of the Most High has risen in our
world, a life has been given us:
— We inherit the Father's Joy!

Antiphon for the 1st Sunday:
Midway through the night, in deep silence,
— Your almighty Word leapt down from heaven.

Antiphon for the Octave:
For the great love that he bore us,
— God sent his Son in flesh like ours.

Antiphon for the 2nd Sunday:
God so loved the world,
that he gave his only Son.

Antiphon for Epiphany:
In the East a star has appeared,
the Magi hail it, full of joy:
This is the sign of the great King,
— Salvation and peace for the nations!

Antiphon of Baptism Sunday:
Sealed with the sign of the Spirit,
Jesus rises from the waters.
The Baptiser knows him and foretells:
— This is the Lamb who gives peace and
    consecrates the world.

Blessed be the Lord God of Israel,
coming to ransom his People;

Raising up saving power
in the house of his servant David,
as he said by the mouth of his prophets,
his saints in the times of old:

He sets us free from oppression,
free from the hands of our foes;
his bond of love with our fathers,
his covenant binding for ever;

His oath to our father Abraham,
assuring us, that liberated from fear,
delivered from all oppression,
we serve him in goodness and love,
before him, throughout our days.

You, child, to be called his prophet,
will walk in the presence of God,
to prepare the ways he shall come,
announcing his People's salvation
with pardon for all their sins.

Through the love in the heart of our God,
the rising Sun will come to us,
shining on those in the dark,
who lie in the shadow of death,
and guiding our steps into peace.

Collect for the day

The Lord be with you, — And also with you.
Let us pray to the Lord: *(silence, then the collect)* — Amen.

Introduction

Blessed be the Lord who alone has worked wonders:
— Blessed be his glorious Name for ever!

———

The Lord has chosen Zion,
— He desired the city for his seat:
This is my rest for ever,
— Here I will reign, it is my will.

———

Glory to God, glory in the highest, Alleluia!
— And peace on earth to all whom he loves, Alleluia!

Psalm

For Christmas, its Octave and Epiphany: Psalm 71
For the Baptism of Christ: Psalm 41

Epistle

Song of Mary

Antiphon of the Nativity:
Marvellous exchange! The creator takes our flesh!
True man, yet owing man nothing,
— God gives us his life, Alleluia!

Antiphon for the 1st Sunday:
Mary kept all these things, and pondered
them in her heart.

Antiphon for the Octave:
Unspeakable mystery! The Virgin the temple
of God! All the nations shall come and say:
— Glory to you, O Lord!

Antiphon for the 2nd Sunday:
The Word became flesh, we have seen his glory.

Antiphon of the Epiphany:
Daughter of Abraham, blessed one,
the Magi worship your Child
and you see the promise fulfilled:
— The joy of earth's nations lies in him.

Antiphon of Baptism Sunday:
What I have done, said the Lord,
you will understand shortly:
I have come to take your sins away:
— Love one another as I have loved you.

My soul sings praises to the Lord,
my spirit glorifies my Saviour, my God!

For he has stooped to his humble servant,
and henceforth all ages will call me greatly blessed.
The Almighty chose me for his wonders;
Holy his Name!

And his love endures through the ages
to all who revere him;
he displays the strength of his arm,
and he scatters the conceited.

He will topple all the powerful from their thrones,
and raise up all the humble.
He feasts all the hungry with good cheer,
sends the rich away empty-handed.

He lifts up his own servant Israel,
ever remembering his love,
his ancient promise made to our fathers
in his oath to Abraham and to his race evermore.

Silence — Hymn

66

Intercession

All the ends of the earth have seen the salvation of our God, Alleluia!
— Acclaim the Lord, all the earth, Alleluia!

January 6:
We have seen his star in the East, Alleluia!
— And we have come to worship him, Alleluia!

———

With joy let us pray to our Saviour, the Son of God made man, and say to him:
— Deliver us, Lord!

By the mystery of your incarnation, by your birth and by your childhood, by your life so fully consecrated:
— Deliver us, Lord!

By your work, by your preaching and travelling, by your friendship with sinners and by all your weariness:
— Deliver us, Lord!

By your agony and your passion, by your cross and your loneliness, by your anguish, by your death and burial:
— Deliver us, Lord!

By your resurrection and by your ascension, by the gift of your Spirit, by your joys and your glory, by our baptism and the eucharist:
— Deliver us, Lord!

Happy the dead who die in the Lord; they rest from their labours for their works follow them; may eternal light shine upon them:
— Deliver us, Lord!

Collect for the day

Free Prayer

General Collect

Lord and Saviour of all mankind; you give salvation to us who can never be worthy of it; purify us of all hypocrisy, that we may freely receive what you freely give; unite us in that bond of peace and love which is the communion of your Body and of your Spirit, as you reign for ever and ever,   — Amen.

Blessing

He was revealed in the flesh,
— Justified in the Spirit,
Contemplated by the angels,
— Proclaimed among the nations,
Believed in the world,
— Taken up into glory!

Let us bless the Lord,
— We give our thanks to God.

May the Lord bless us, the Maker of heaven and earth.
— Amen.

Introduction

Blessed be the Lord who alone has worked wonders:
— Blessed be his glorious Name for ever!

———

God reigns! Let the earth exult,
— And all the islands rejoice;
Darkness and cloud surround him,
— His throne is justice and truth.

Light arises for the righteous,
— And joy for the upright heart;
Rejoice, you righteous, in the Lord,
— Praise the memory of his holiness.

———

For us a child is born, to us the Son is given, Alleluia!
— All the ends of the earth have seen the salvation of our
    God, Alleluia!

Psalm — Old Testament

Responses

Begotten of the Father before the dawn,
+ You are made Master on the day of your birth.
— Begotten of the Father . . .

A word from the Lord to my Master: Sit at my side,
your enemies shall be your footstool:
— You are made Master on the day of your birth.

From Zion the Lord will wield a sceptre of power
and rule in the midst of the enemy.
— You are made Master on the day of your birth.

Lord on the holy mountains from the day you were born,
begotten of my love with the dawning ages.
— You are made Master . . .

The Lord has sworn and will not change:
you are for ever priest, as Melchizedek was.
— You are made Master . . .

Glory to the Father, and the Son and the Holy Spirit.
— Begotten of the Father. . . .

Gospel — Silence

Intercession

The Lord has shown salvation, Alleluia!
— He has revealed his justice, Alleluia!

———

With joy let us pray to our Saviour, the Son of God made man
and say to him:
— Lord, blessed be your Name.

O Christ, Son of God, you were before the world began, and
you came to save us all: making us witnesses of your goodness.
— Lord, blessed be your Name.

Sun of justice, you shone in all eternity, true light of all that
exists: giving light to all who dwell in the shadow of death.
— Lord, blessed be your Name.

You became a tiny child and were laid in a manger: showing
us the simplicity of the Father's love.
— Lord, blessed be your Name.

King of glory, you accepted such inconceivable humbling: to
show us the spirit of our discipleship.
— Lord, blessed be your Name.

You became living Bread for us and gave us eternal life:
gladden our hearts as we celebrate the eucharist.
— Lord, blessed be your Name.

Collect for the week

The Lord be with you, — And also with you.
Let us pray to the Lord: *(silence, then the collect)* — Amen.

Free Prayer

General Collect

Glory to you, our Lord Jesus Christ; in love the Father begot you, and in love you make yourself known to all who celebrate you. In you is our beginning, and in you our hope and desires find their fulfilment. So deliver us from the sadness of doubt and fear; may the secret of your birth and the glory of your cross always remain in our minds; for your light shines in our darkness and nothing shall separate us from the power of your love, now or ever,   — Amen.

The Lord's Prayer

O Christ, remember us in your Kingdom,
— Lord, teach us to pray: Our Father . . .

Blessing

Let us bless the Lord,
— We give our thanks to God.

May grace be with all who love our Lord Jesus Christ in unending life.
— Amen.

Introduction

Blessed be the Lord who alone has worked wonders:
— Blessed be his glorious Name for ever!

———

The angel of the Lord appeared to the shepherds,
— And glory surrounded them with its brightness:
Good news I bring, and great joy
— To you and to all peoples:
Today a Saviour is born for you,
— He is Christ the Lord.

———

Glory to God, glory in the highest, Alleluia!
— And peace on earth to all whom he loves, Alleluia!

Psalm — Epistle

Responses

The Word was made flesh, Alleluia, Alleluia!
— The Word . . .

He dwelt among us.
— Alleluia, Alleluia!

Glory to the Father, and the Son and the Holy Spirit.
— The Word was made flesh, Alleluia, Alleluia!

Silence — Hymn

Intercession

All the ends of the earth have seen the salvation of our God,
Alleluia!
— Acclaim the Lord, all the earth, Alleluia!

———

Lord, have mercy!
— Christ, have mercy!

Lord, have mercy!
— Christ, hear us!

God, the Father of heaven,
— Mercy for us!

God the Son, Redeemer of the world,
— Mercy for us!

God, the Holy Spirit,
— Mercy for us!

God, one God, thrice holy,
— Mercy for us!

With the angels and archangels, and with the souls of all the
blessed, Lord, we praise you:
— Glory to God in the highest!

With the patriarchs and prophets, Lord, we bless you:
— Glory to God in the highest!

With the Virgin Mary, Mother of our Lord, our souls magnify
the Lord:
— Glory to God in the highest!

With the Apostles and evangelists, Lord, we give you thanks:
— Glory to God in the highest!

With all the martyrs of Christ, Lord, we offer you our bodies
in sacrifice:
— Glory to God in the highest!

With all the holy witnesses to the Gospel, Lord, we consecrate
our lives:
— Glory to God in the highest!

With all your People of the Church throughout the world,
Lord, we worship you:
— Glory to God in the highest!

Happy the dead who die in the Lord and rest now from their
labours for their works follow them:
— Glory to God in the highest!

Collect for the week

The Lord be with you, — And also with you.
Let us pray to the Lord: *(silence, then the collect)* — Amen.

Free Prayer

General Collect

God of mercy; because you showed your power in the incarnation and resurrection of our Lord, your saints triumphed in
suffering and death. Strengthen us, too, that we may run our
race in faith until we receive together the crown of unending
life, through Jesus Christ, your Son, our Lord,   — Amen.

Blessing

He was revealed in the flesh,
— Justified in the Spirit,
Contemplated by the angels,
— Proclaimed among the nations,
Believed in the world,
— Taken up into glory!

Let us bless the Lord,
— We give our thanks to God.

May the Lord of peace give us peace in all ways and at all
times.
— Amen.

Introduction

Blessed be the Lord who alone has worked wonders:
— Blessed be his glorious Name for ever!

———

Such love in the heart of our God!
— The rising Sun has come to us,
Shining on those in the dark,
— Who lie in the shadow of death;

Guiding our steps into peace,
— A lamp shining in the darkness,
Until day begins to dawn
— And the morning-star rises in our hearts.

———

For us a child is born, to us the Son is given, Alleluia!
— All the ends of the earth have seen the salvation of our
    God, Alleluia!

Psalm — Old Testament

Responses

He sends his Word upon earth,
 + Swiftly runs his Truth.
— He sends his Word . . .

He gives peace to your land for ever,
feeds you with the finest wheat.
— Swiftly . . .

He flings down hail like stones;
who can withstand his cold?
— Swiftly . . .

He send his Word of warmth,
he blows with his wind and the waters flow.
— Swiftly . . .

He reveals his Word to Jacob,
his laws and judgements to Israel.
— Swiftly . . .

Glory to the Father, and the Son and the Holy Spirit.
— He sends his Word . . .

Gospel — Silence

Intercession

Our help is in the name of the Lord, Alleluia!
— Who made heaven and earth, Alleluia!

———

With joy let us pray to our Saviour, the Son of God made man
and say to him:
— Son of the living God, have mercy on us.

O Christ, splendour of the Father's glory! Sustaining all the
worlds by your Word of power: we pray that our lives may
ever be renewed by your presence.
— Son of the living God, have mercy on us.

O Christ, born into the world in the fulness of time for the
salvation and liberation of every creature: we pray that all
may come to their rightful freedom.
— Son of the living God, have mercy on us.

O Christ, begotten of the Father before all time, born in the
stable at Bethlehem: we pray that your Church may be a sign
of poverty and joy.
— Son of the living God, have mercy on us.

O Christ, true God and true man, born in a People to fulfil
their expectations: may all find their desires fulfilled in you.
— Son of the living God, have mercy on us.

O Christ, child of the Virgin Mary, wonderful in Counsel, mighty Lord, eternal God, Prince of Peace: we pray that the whole world may live in peace and justice.
— Son of the living God, have mercy on us.

Collect for the week

The Lord be with you, — And also with you.
Let us pray to the Lord: *(silence, then the collect)* — Amen.

Free Prayer

General Collect

Lord Christ, your light shines in our darkness, giving gladness in our sorrow and a presence in our isolation; we pray you to fill our lives with your mystery, until our hearts overflow with gladness and praise, for you are the beginning and end of all that exists, and you live for evermore,   — Amen.

The Lord's Prayer

O Christ, remember us in your Kingdom,
— Lord, teach us to pray: Our Father ...

Blessing

Let us bless the Lord,
— We give our thanks to God.

May the God of peace sanctify us wholly, keeping us blameless in body, mind and soul for the Coming of our Lord Jesus Christ.
— Amen.

Introduction

Blessed be the Lord who alone has worked wonders:
— Blessed be his glorious Name for ever!

———

You shall know that I am the Lord, your Saviour,
— The Mighty One of Jacob, your Redeemer;
For the Lord will be your everlasting light,
— And your God your glory.

Your sun will set no more,
— And your moon no more withdraw,
For the Lord will be your everlasting light,
— And the days of your mourning fulfilled.

———

Glory to God, glory in the highest, Alleluia!
— And peace on earth to all whom he loves, Alleluia!

Psalm — Epistle

Responses

The Word was made flesh, Alleluia, Alleluia!
— The Word ...

He dwelt among us!
— Alleluia, Alleluia!

Glory to the Father, and the Son and the Holy Spirit.
— The Word ...

Silence — Hymn

Intercession

Blessed be the name of the Lord, Alleluia!
— From henceforth and for ever, Alleluia!

Almighty God, you have never forsaken the world when it abandoned you; from ancient times you made the promise of your victory shine before your People:
— The joy of our hearts is in God!

The patriarchs hoped for your Christ, Abraham rejoiced to see his day, foretold by the prophets and desired by all the nations:
— The joy of our hearts is in God!

The heavenly host celebrated his birth; apostles, martyrs and the faithful throughout the ages have repeated the angels' song, and now we with your whole Church praise you; for our eyes have seen your salvation:
— The joy of our hearts is in God!

Son of God, you became poor to make many rich; you humbled yourself and took the form of a slave, lifting us up to share in your glory.
— The joy of our hearts is in God!

We were in darkness and you have given us light and strength; we were without hope and we have received from your fulness grace upon grace.
— The joy of our hearts is in God!

Dispose of us as you will; make us a People who serve you in holiness; give us honest hearts to hear your word and produce in us abundant fruit to your glory.
— The joy of our hearts is in God!

Collect for the week

The Lord be with you, — And also with you.
Let us pray to the Lord: *(silence, then the collect)* — Amen.

Free Prayer

General Collect

O God; so great was your love for the world, that you gave your only Son for us. Ground our belief so firmly in the mystery of your Word made flesh, that we may find in him victory over all evil, for he reigns now and for ever, — Amen.

Blessing

He was revealed in the flesh,
— Justified by the Spirit,
Contemplated by the angels,
— Proclaimed among the nations,
Believed in the world,
— Taken up into glory!

Let us bless the Lord,
— We give our thanks to God.

May the grace of our Lord Jesus Christ, the love of God and the communion of the Holy Spirit be with us all.
— Amen.

Introduction

Blessed be the Lord who alone has worked wonders:
— Blessed be his glorious Name for ever!

―――

The earth has yielded its harvest
— God, our God has blessed us.
Before him all kings shall bow down,
— And all nations shall serve him.

All peoples shall come and worship,
— O Master, they will glorify your name.
For you are great and you do great wonders,
— You, God, you alone.

―――

For us a child is born, to us the Son is given, Alleluia!
— All the ends of the world have seen the salvation of our
God, Alleluia!

Psalm — Old Testament

Responses

Arise, shine, for your light has come!
+ The glory of the Lord has risen upon you.
— Arise, shine . . .

The Lord rises upon you and his glory appears over you.
— The glory of the Lord has risen upon you.

The nations come to your light,
and kings to the brightness of your rising.
— The glory . . .

Lift up your eyes and see,
they all gather and move towards you.
— The glory . . .

People from Sheba will come, bearing gold and incense,
singing the praise of God.
— The glory . . .

Glory to the Father, and the Son and the Holy Spirit.
— Arise, shine . . .

Gospel — Silence

Intercession

Fall down before him, Alleluia!
— All his angels, Alleluia!

_____

O Christ, by your epiphany light has shone on us, giving us
the fulness of salvation: grant your light to all we shall
encounter today:
— Kyrie eleison (*or*: Lord, have mercy).

O Christ, you humbled yourself and received baptism at your
servant's hands, showing us the way of humility: grant us to
serve humbly all the days of our life:
— Kyrie eleison.

O Christ, by your baptism you washed away every impurity,
making us children of the Father: grant the grace of Son-ship
to all who are searching for you:
— Kyrie eleison.

O Christ, by your baptism you sanctified the creation and
opened the way of repentance to all who are baptised: make
us instruments of your Gospel in the world:
— Kyrie eleison.

O Christ, by your baptism you revealed the Trinity, your
Father calling you his beloved Son, through the Spirit descend-
ing upon you: renew a heart of worship in the royal priesthood
of all the baptised.
— Kyrie eleison.

Collect for the week

The Lord be with you, — And also with you.
Let us pray to the Lord: *(silence, then the collect)* — Amen.

Free Prayer

General Collect

O Christ, light made manifest as the true light of God; gladden our hearts on the joyful morning of your glory, call us by our name on the great Day of your coming and give us grace to offer unending praise with all the hosts of heaven to the Father in whom all things find their ending, now and ever, — Amen.

The Lord's Prayer

O Christ, remember us in your Kingdom,
— Lord, teach us to pray: Our Father . . .

Blessing

Let us bless the Lord,
— We give our thanks to God.

May the Lord bless us and keep us; may Christ smile upon us and give us his grace; may he unveil his face to us and bring us his peace.
— Amen.

Introduction

Blessed be the Lord who alone has worked wonders:
— Blessed be his glorious Name for ever.

———

Lift up your eyes and see,
— They all gather and move towards you.
At that sight you will be radiant,
— Your heart overflowing with joy.

People from Sheba will come, bearing gold and incense,
— Singing the praises of God.
I will make you an eternal honour,
— A source of joy for ever and ever.

———

Glory to God, glory in the highest, Alleluia!
— And peace on earth to all whom he loves, Alleluia!

Psalm — Epistle

Responses

They come hurrying from far and wide, Alleluia, Alleluia!
— They come hurrying . . .

Bringing gold, and frankincense, and myrrh,
— Alleluia, Alleluia!

Glory to the Father, and the Son and the Holy Spirit.
— They come hurrying . . .

Silence — Hymn

Intercession

We have seen his star in the East, Alleluia!
— And we have come to worship him, Alleluia!

With joy let us pray to our Saviour, the Son of God made man, and say to him:
— The grace of God be with us all.

O Christ, sow everywhere your word of life: draw every creature to yourself:
— The grace of God be with us all.

O Christ, Saviour and Lord, extend your Church on every side: make us a place of welcome for every person:
— The grace of God be with us all.

Sun of Justice, direct the working and thinking of statesmen and rulers everywhere: give peace and freedom to every nation.
— The grace of God be with us all.

Master of all, courage for the weak and comfort for the distressed, strengthen and lift us up, watch over all who are lonely or threatened: sustain the faith and hope of those persecuted.
— The grace of God be with us all.

Happy the dead who die in the Lord; they rest from their labours for their works follow them: may eternal light shine on them.
— The grace of God be with us all.

Collect for the week

The Lord be with you, — And also with you.
Let us pray to the Lord: *(silence, then the collect)* — Amen.

Free Prayer

General Collect

Lord Jesus, you said: Ask and you will receive, the door will be opened; give our hearts such love that our whole lives be inspired by it, in all that we do, and that we never tire of praising you with the Father and the Holy Spirit now and for ever,   — Amen.

Blessing

He was revealed in the flesh,
— Justified in the Spirit,
Contemplated by the angels,
— Proclaimed among the nations,
Believed in the world,
— Taken up into glory!

Let us bless the Lord,
— We give our thanks to God.

May our Lord Jesus Christ himself, and God our Father who
has loved us, and given us by his grace eternal consolation and
joyful hope, comfort our hearts and strengthen them in every
good word and work.
— Amen.

*From the Monday morning after Baptism Sunday (1st after
Epiphany Sunday) until Shrove Tuesday the liturgy for
Ordinary Days is used.*

Lent

The season of Lent is a time of spiritual retreat for the whole Church. The liturgy prepares us more specifically to celebrate our liberation.

In communion with Christ in the desert, the Church is invited to forty days of purification, of stripping down to bare essentials, of discipline, meditation and prayer before the Festival of Easter.

These forty days are a celebration of our joy in the Father's forgiveness.

SUNDAY MORNING

Introduction

Lend an ear, O Lord, and answer me,
— Poor and wretched as I am;
Keep my soul, I am your friend,
— Save your servant who trusts in you.

You are my God; Master, have pity,
— I call on you all the day;
O my Master, gladden your servant,
— For I lift up my soul to you.

Master, you are pardon and kindness,
— Full of love for all who pray;
Lord, hear my prayer,
— Listen to the voice of my pleading.

Psalm 129

Short Reading

This day is holy to the Lord, your God! Leave your mourning, leave your weeping, for this day is holy to our Lord! Leave your lamentations; the joy of the Lord is our rampart.

Song of Zechariah *(see Sunday Mornings in Advent)*
Antiphon: Blessed is he who comes in the name of the Lord.

Collect for the week

The Lord be with you, — And also with you.
Let us pray to the Lord: *(silence, then the collect)* — Amen.

SUNDAY EVENING

Introduction

Return to the Lord your God,
— For he is tenderness and compassion.

In the day of distress I call,
— For you answer me, Master;
Among the gods, there is none like you,
— Nothing to approach your works.

All nations will come and worship,
— Master, they will praise your name;
For you are great and you do great wonders,
— You, God, and you alone.

Worthy is the Lamb that was slain
to receive power and riches and wisdom,
— Strength, honour, glory and praise. Amen.

Psalm — Epistle

Song of Mary *(see Sunday Evening in Advent)*
Antiphon: The glory of your cross lightens the world,
Christ, our Saviour, we give you thanks.

Silence — Hymn

Intercession

The angels will bear you in their hands,
— Your foot will not stumble on a stone.

———

Lord have mercy,
— Christ mave mercy.

Lord have mercy,
— Christ hear us.

God the Father in heaven,
— Mercy for us!

God the Son, Redeemer of the world,
— Mercy for us!

God the Holy Spirit,
— Mercy for us!

God, one God, thrice holy,
— Mercy for us!

O Christ, of your fulness we have all received. You are our eternal hope. You are patient and full of kindness. You are generous to all who call upon you.
— Intercede for us!

O Christ, fountain of life and of holiness. You have taken away our sins. You were loaded with insults and crushed beneath the burden of our faults.
— Intercede for us!

O Christ, obedient unto death, source of all comfort, our life and our resurrection, our peace and our reconciliation.
— Intercede for us!

O Christ, salvation of all who hope in you, hope of all who die in you, and bliss of all the saints.
— Intercede for us!

Lamb of God, you take away the sin of the world,
— Lord forgive!

Lamb of God, you take away the sin of the world,
— Lord hear us!

Lamb of God, you take away the sin of the world,
— Lord have mercy on us!

Jesus, gentle and humble of heart,
— Give us hearts like yours.

Collect for the week

The Lord be with you, — And also with you.
Let us pray to the Lord: *(silence, then the collect)* — Amen.

Free Prayer

General Collect

Lord, in your kindness, hear the prayers of all who confess their wretchedness. When conscience accuses us of sin, may your pardon assure us of our liberation, through Jesus Christ, your Son, our Lord.   — Amen.

Blessing

After his spirit has been tested,
— The Servant will see light and be comforted;
By his sufferings he will justify thousands,
— Taking their faults upon himself.

Let us bless the Lord,
— We give our thanks to God.

May the Lord bless us, the Maker of heaven and earth.
— Amen.

MONDAY MORNING

Introduction

Return to the Lord, he has pity on you,
— To God, he is all forgiveness.

O Lord, teach me your ways,
— That I may walk in your truth.
Mould my heart to love you,
— For you comfort and help me.

Master, I thank you with all my heart,
— Glory to your Name for ever,
Your love for me is boundless,
— You have raised me from the depths.

To him who reigns from the throne, and to the Lamb.
— Praise and honour, glory and power for ever and ever.
  Amen.

Psalm — Old Testament

Responses

Return, O Lord. Deliver my soul.
 + Save me, for the sake of your love.
— Return, O Lord . . .

Have pity on me, my strength is gone,
heal me, my bones are broken.
— Save me, for the sake of your love.

My soul is in deep distress;
Lord, how long till you return?
— Save me . . .

The Lord hears my petition,
the Lord will receive my prayer.
— Save me . . .

My enemies, routed and confounded,
will suddenly retreat in confusion.
— Save me ...

Glory to the Father, and the Son and the Holy Spirit.
— Return, O Lord ...

Gospel — Silence

Intercession

He has charged his angels
— To keep you in all your ways.

Lord, we pray you to inspire continually your Church universal with the Spirit of truth, unity and peace.
— Remember your love, O Lord.

Give your grace to all bishops and pastors, that by their life and their faith they may show forth your Word of Truth and celebrate your sacraments in love and in joy.
— Remember ...

Give your grace to all your People, and to us met together in your presence; may we hear and receive your Word with purity of heart and true obedience, to serve you all the days of our life.
— Remember ...

We pray you to give your guidance to all who govern us, disposing their hearts to lead us in peace, according to your will: grant that they may truly seek after justice.
— Remember ...

We implore you to help and comfort all who live in trouble, sadness, want or sickness.
— Remember ...

We bless your holy Name for all your servants who have passed from this life in faith and in obedience. We pray for grace to follow their example and to share with them in your Kingdom.
— Remember . . .

Collect for the week

The Lord be with you, — And also with you.
Let us pray to the Lord: *(silence, then the collect)* — Amen.

Free Prayer

General Collect

O God, you have brought us out of the darkness of night into the brightness of morning; by your Holy Spirit, dispel the darkness of sin and doubt. In your goodness, pour such light into our hearts, that they may be yours without fear of separation, through Jesus Christ our Lord, — Amen.

The Lord's Prayer

O Christ, remember us in your Kingdom,
— Lord, teach us to pray: Our Father . . .

Blessing

Let us bless the Lord,
— We give our thanks to God.

May the God of hope fill us with all joy and all peace in believing, that we may be overflowing with hope through the power of the Holy Spirit.
— Amen.

MONDAY EVENING

Introduction

Return to the Lord, your God,
— For he is tenderness and compassion.

O God of tenderness and compassion,
— O Master, slow to anger,
Full of love and full of truth,
— Turn towards me, have compassion.

Give your strength to your servant,
— And salvation to the child of your People;
Give me a sign of your kindness
— For Lord, you help and comfort me.

Worthy is the Lamb that was slain
to receive power and riches and wisdom,
— Strength, honour, glory and praise. Amen.

Psalm — Epistle

Responses

From the snare of the hunter, he will deliver you.
— From the snare . . .

He will cover you with his wings,
— He will deliver you.

Glory to the Father, and the Son and the Holy Spirit.
— From the snare . . .

Silence — Hymn

Intercession

The angels will bear you in their hands,
— Your foot will not stumble on a stone.

We call upon you, Lord God; you know everything, nothing escapes from you, Master of all truth:
— Be my rock and my fortress, O Lord!

You have made all the worlds and you watch over every creature. You guide to the way of life all who are living in darkness and the shadow of death:
— Be my rock ...

It is your will to save everyone in the world, and to bring them to fulness. We offer you our praise and thanks, glorifying you with heart and voice.
— Be my rock ...

It was your will to call us, instructing us and opening the way for us to follow. You have given us wisdom and understanding for life eternal:
— Be my rock ...

You have ransomed us by the precious blood of your only Son, in spite of all our wanderings, from the slavery of sin, and you have given us glory and freedom:
— Be my rock ...

We were dead and you gave us new birth by the Spirit. We were sinners and you gave us pure hearts.
— Be my rock ...

Collect for the week

The Lord be with you, — And also with you.
Let us pray to the Lord: *(silence, then the collect)* — Amen.

Free Prayer

General Collect

Eternal God, you know what for us is hidden; bless your People as we lay before you the hardness of our hearts. Strengthen us in your might, deliver us from all that is evil and confirm us in faith, through Jesus Christ, our Lord,
— Amen.

Blessing

After his spirit has been tested,
— The Servant will see light and be comforted;
By his sufferings he will justify thousands,
— Taking their faults upon himself.

Let us bless the Lord,
— We give our thanks to God.

May the God of peace sanctify us wholly, keeping us blameless in body, mind and soul for the Coming of our Lord Jesus Christ.
— Amen.

TUESDAY MORNING

Introduction

Return to the Lord, he has pity on you,
— To God, he is all forgiveness.

What joy when our sin is forgiven,
— Our faults remitted!
What joy when God the Lord
— Clears us of wrong!

I kept silence and my bones were consumed
— In groaning all the day;
Night and day your hand
— Weighed heavy upon me.

My heart turned to straw
— In the blaze of summer;
I laid bare my fault,
— I did not hide my sin.

I said: I will go to the Lord
— And confess my fault;
And you have absolved me from wrong,
— Pardoning all my sin.

To him who reigns from the throne, and to the Lamb,
— Praise and honour, glory and power for ever and ever.
  Amen.

Psalm — Old Testament

Responses

O Master, all my desire is before you.
+ My sighing for you is not hidden.
— O Master . . .

It is for you, Lord, that I hope,
it is you who will reply, God my Master.
— My sighing . . .

I do confess my offences,
I am concerned for my fault.
— My sighing . . .

Never abandon me, Lord,
my God, be not far from me.
— My sighing . . .

Come quickly to my help,
God, my Master and my Saviour.
— My sighing . . .

Glory to the Father, and the Son and the Holy Spirit.
— O Master . . .

Gospel — Silence

Intercession

He has charged his angels,
— To keep you in all your ways.

God our Father, you are the maker of heaven and earth:
— Be our freedom, Lord!

God the Son, you redeem us all:
— Be our freedom, Lord!

God, Holy Spirit, you sanctify our lives:
— Be our freedom, Lord!

God, one God, thrice holy:
— Be our freedom, Lord!

By your Incarnation and your birth in poverty, by your baptism, your fasting and your trials in the desert:
— Be our freedom, Lord!

By your agony in the garden, by your Cross and Passion, by your death and your burial, by your resurrection and ascension, and by the gifts of your Holy Spirit:
— Be our freedom, Lord!

In times of trouble, and when all goes well, at the hour we die and on the Day of your glory:
— Be our freedom, Lord!

From war and violence, from hardness of heart and from contempt of your love and your promises:
— Be our freedom, Lord!

Enlighten our lives with your Word, that in it we may find our way and our hope:
— Be our freedom, Lord!

Assist your people in every land, govern them in peace and justice, defend them from the enemies of life:
— Be our freedom, Lord!

Collect for the week

The Lord be with you, — And also with you.
Let us pray to the Lord: *(silence, then the collect)* — Amen.

Free Prayer

General Collect

O Christ, Son of God, may we always share in your love; and since you gave your life for us, may your Passion help us in all the trials of our existence, making of us true and living members of your Body, for you live and reign now and for ever,   — Amen.

The Lord's Prayer

O Christ, remember us in your Kingdom,
— Lord, teach us to pray: Our Father . . .

Blessing

Let us bless the Lord,
— We give our thanks to God.

May the Lord bless us and keep us; may Christ smile upon us and give us his grace; may he unveil his face to us and bring us his peace.
— Amen.

TUESDAY EVENING

Introduction

Return to the Lord, your God,
— For he is tenderness and compassion.

My fault I have laid before you,
— I did not hide my sin;
I said: I will go to the Lord
— And confess my fault.

Lord, you have absolved me,
— Forgiving my sin;
Each child of yours invokes you
— In the hour of distress.

Should the great rivers overflow,
— They cannot reach me;
You are a refuge for me,
— You keep me from distress.

Worthy is the Lamb that was slain
to receive power and riches and wisdom,
— Strength, honour, glory and praise. Amen.

Psalm — Epistle

Responses

More mighty than armour, the Lord is beside you.
— More mighty . . .

You will not fear the terrors of night,
— The Lord is beside you.

Glory to the Father, and the Son and the Holy Spirit.
— More mighty . . .

Silence — Hymn

Intercession

The angels will bear you in their hands,
— Your foot will not stumble on a stone.

With one heart and with one voice let us pray to the Lord
God almighty:
— Lord, have mercy.

Look down on us from your holy place:
— Lord, have mercy.

On your Church universal in every country:
— Lord . . .

On all her bishops, pastors and people:
— Lord . . .

On this land and all who live here:
— Lord . . .

Grant good weather and good harvests:
— Lord . . .

We know your strength and your kindness:
— Lord . . .

In your love, grant us freedom:
— Lord . . .

Collect for the week

The Lord be with you, — And also with you.
Let us pray to the Lord: *(silence, then the collect)* — Amen.

Free Prayer

General Collect

Almighty God, from whom all holy desires, all good counsels and all just works proceed; give us, your servants, that peace which the world cannot give, that our hearts may be set to serve you faithfully, and be ever free to praise you with joy, through Jesus Christ our Lord,   — Amen.

Blessing

After his spirit has been tested,
— The Servant will see light and be comforted;
By his sufferings he will justify thousands,
— Taking their faults upon himself.

Let us bless the Lord,
— We give our thanks to God.

May the Lord of peace give us peace in all ways and at all times.
— Amen.

WEDNESDAY MORNING

Introduction

Return to the Lord, he has pity on you,
— To God, he is all forgiveness.

Pity me, Lord, in your kindness,
— In your love blot out my sin;
Wash me of all my faults,
— Cleanse me from my misdeeds.

For I know my sin,
— My fault is ever before me.
Against you, you only, I have sinned.
— I have done evil in your sight.

To him who reigns from the throne, and to the Lamb,
— Praise and honour, glory and power for ever and ever.
Amen.

Psalm — Old Testament

Responses

Incline your ear to me,
+ And answer me when I call.
— Incline . . .

Lord, hear my prayer,
let my cry come unto you.
— And answer . . .

Hide not your face far from me
in the day when anguish takes hold.
— And answer . . .

Lord, you reign for ever;
age after age recalls you.
— And answer . . .

You will rise in pity for your People,
longing to show them your mercy.
— And answer . . .

Glory to the Father, and the Son and the Holy Spirit.
— Incline your ear . . .

Gospel — Silence

Intercession
He has charged his angels
— To keep you in all your ways.

Lord, give your People grace to hear your Word, to receive
it with a pure heart and to bring forth the fruits of the Spirit.
— Hear us, O Lord.

Help and comfort all who are in danger, need and trouble.
— Hear . . .

Protect the sick and show your compassion to prisoners.
— Hear . . .

Defend orphans, widows and all who are sad and oppressed.
Provide for all their needs.
— Hear . . .

Grant us joy and thankfulness for your ceaseless gifts to us all.
— Hear . . .

Give us true repentance by your Holy Spirit, that we may
change our lives according to your Word.
— Hear . . .

Collect for the week
The Lord be with you, — And also with you.
Let us pray to the Lord: *(silence, then the collect)* — Amen.

Free Prayer

General Collect

O God, the light of your glory shines in the darkness of our lives. Make us attentive to your presence, prompt to serve you and ever eager to follow in the steps of the One who is the true light and the source of life, Jesus Christ, your Son, our Lord,   — Amen.

The Lord's Prayer

O Christ, remember us in your Kingdom,
— Lord, teach us to pray: Our Father . . .

Blessing

Let us bless the Lord,
— We give our thanks to God.

May the God of patience and of consolation grant us to live together after the pattern of our Lord Jesus Christ, so that with one heart and one voice we may give glory to God, the Father of our Lord Jesus Christ.
— Amen.

WEDNESDAY EVENING

Introduction

Return to the Lord, your God,
— For he is tenderness and compassion.

You love truth in the inmost heart,
— Teach me the depths of wisdom;
Cleanse me with hyssop; I shall be clean;
— Wash me: I shall be whiter than snow.

Restore the sound of joy and festival,
— Make the bones you have broken dance;
Turn your face from my faults,
— Blot out all my sins.

Worthy is the Lamb that was slain
to receive power and riches and wisdom,
— Strength, honour, glory and praise. Amen.

Psalm — Epistle

Responses

With his wings, he will cover you.
— With his wings . . .

And under his feathers you will find rest and shelter,
— He will cover you.

Glory to the Father, and the Son and the Holy Spirit.
— With his wings . . .

Silence — Hymn

Intercession

The angels will bear you in their hands,
— Your foot will not stumble on a stone.

Faithful friend, stretch out your strong hand to all who are in danger and distress; sustain by your Father's Word, which nourished you in the desert, all who are in prison for their faith.
— Have mercy, Lord.

Bring an end to wars and bloodshed; preserve peace for us and give salvation and happiness to the whole world.
— Have mercy, Lord.

Have pity on us all; guard and bless travellers; comfort the afflicted; support the aged and care for the sick.
— Have mercy, Lord.

When you call us to leave this world, give us grace to trust in your redeeming love.
— Have mercy, Lord.

You died for us that we might die to sin; you rose for us that we might have eternal life.
— Have mercy, Lord.

Collect for the week

The Lord be with you, — And also with you.
Let us pray to the Lord: *(silence, then the collect)* — Amen.

Free Prayer

General Collect

Comfort, Lord, all who cry to you. Transform the sorrows of our faults into the joy of pardon, and in your goodness hasten for us the return of Jesus Christ, our Lord,   — Amen.

Blessing

After his spirit has been tested,
— The Servant will see light and be comforted;
By his sufferings he will justify thousands,
— Taking their faults upon himself.

Let us bless the Lord,
— We give our thanks to God.

May our Lord Jesus Christ himself, and God our Father who has loved us, and given us by his grace eternal consolation and joyful hope, comfort our hearts and strengthen them in every good word and work.
— Amen.

THURSDAY MORNING

Introduction

Return to the Lord, he has pity on you,
— To God, he is all forgiveness.

O God, create in me a pure heart,
— Restore in me a strong spirit;
Cast me not away from your presence,
— Nor withdraw your Holy Spirit.

Renew in me the joy of your salvation,
— Endue me with a generous spirit;
I will teach your ways to sinners,
— And the lost will return to you.

To him who reigns from the throne, and to the Lamb,
— Praise and honour, glory and power for ever and ever.
    Amen.

Psalm — Old Testament

Responses: *As Monday Morning*

Gospel — Silence

Intercession

He has charged his angels,
— To keep you in all your ways.

Lord, we pray . . . *(As Monday Morning)*

Collect for the week

The Lord be with you, — And also with you.
Let us pray to the Lord: *(silence, then the collect)* — Amen.

Free Prayer

General Collect

God our Father, you so loved the world that you sent your only Son to be our Salvation. Kindle in our hearts that same love with which Christ loves us, now and for ever,   — Amen.

The Lord's Prayer

O Christ, remember us in your Kingdom,
— Lord, teach us to pray: Our Father . . .

Blessing

Let us bless the Lord,
— We give our thanks to God.

May the God of peace enable us to do his will in every kind of goodness, working in us what pleases him, through Jesus Christ, to whom be the glory for ever and ever.
— Amen.

THURSDAY EVENING

Introduction

Return to the Lord, your God,
— For he is tenderness and compassion.

You would show no pleasure in sacrifice,
— If I offered a burnt offering, you would not take it:
My sacrifice is a broken spirit,
— The broken heart you never despise.

Grant happiness to Zion,
— And build up the walls of Jerusalem.
You will love true sacrifices,
— Total self-giving at your altar.

Worthy is the Lamb that was slain
to receive power and riches and wisdom,
— Strength, honour, glory and praise. Amen.

Psalm — Epistle

Responses: *As Monday Evening*

Silence — Hymn

Intercession

The angels will bear you in their hands,
— Your foot will not stumble on a stone.

Father of mercy, God of all consolation, strengthen us in our
vocation to adore and to serve you faithfully.
— Save us, Lord of all.

We would now draw near and consecrate ourselves to your
Word and to your perfect Will. Enlighten our hearts to know
and to love you.
— Save us . . .

Give us strength to do what we have to do, and do not remember the sins we commit.
— Save us . . .

Remember how easily we fall; your followers are weak by nature, weak in ability, and the evil in us is hidden.
— Save us . . .

Strengthen us with your strength; give to us all the light of your consoling presence.
— Save us . . .

Conform us to the truth of your Word in faith, keep us obedient to the apostles' teaching of the Gospel of our Saviour, Jesus Christ.
— Save us . . .

Collect for the week

The Lord be with you, — And also with you.
Let us pray to the Lord: *(silence, then the collect)* — Amen.

Free Prayer

General Collect

O God and Father of mercy, receive the prayers we offer in our times of need, and keep our hearts in constant thankfulness, through Jesus Christ our Lord,   — Amen.

Blessing

After his spirit has been tested,
— The Servant will see light and be comforted;
By his sufferings he will justify thousands,
— Taking their faults upon himself.

Let us bless the Lord,
— We give our thanks to God.

May the grace of our Lord Jesus Christ, the love of God and
the communion of the Holy Spirit be with us all.
—Amen.

FRIDAY MORNING

Introduction

Return to the Lord, he has pity on you,
— To God, he is all forgiveness.

From the depths I call to you, O Lord:
— Hear my cry!
Let your ear be attentive
— To the words of my prayer.

If you should retain our faults,
— Lord, who could stand?
But with you there is forgiveness:
— I worship and I hope.

My soul waits for the Lord,
— I am sure of his Word;
My soul relies on the Lord,
— More than a watchman on the dawn.

Since grace is found with the Lord,
— And the fullest of ransoms,
It is he who will ransom Israel
— From all his faults.

To him who reigns from the throne, and to the Lamb,
— Praise and honour, glory and power for ever and ever.
Amen.

Psalm — Old Testament

Responses: *As Tuesday Morning*

Gospel — Silence

Intercession: *As Tuesday Morning*

Collect for the week

The Lord be with you, — And also with you.
Let us pray to the Lord: *(silence, then the collect)* — Amen.

Free Prayer

General Collect

Father, you see how weak we are; grant us to put our trust in your loving mercy, and serve you in singleness of heart, through Jesus our Lord, — Amen.

The Lord's Prayer

O Christ, remember us in your Kingdom,
— Lord, teach us to pray: Our Father . . .

Blessing

Let us bless the Lord,
— We give our thanks to God.

May God the Father, and our Lord Jesus Christ, grant us peace and love, in believing.
— Amen.

FRIDAY EVENING

Introduction

Return to the Lord your God,
— For he is tenderness and compassion.

Lord, hear my prayer,
— You are faithful, answer me, you are just.
Do not bring your servant to judgement:
— No one is justified before you.

The enemy pursues my life,
— He fells me to the ground.
He makes me dwell in darkness,
— Like those who are dead for ever.

The breath in my body fails,
— My heart in my breast is fearful.
Deliver me from all my enemies,
— Lord, I flee to your mercy.

Worthy is the Lamb that was slain
to receive power and riches and wisdom,
— Strength, honour, glory and praise. Amen.

Psalm — Epistle

Responses: *As Tuesday Evening*

Silence — Hymn

Intercession

The angels will bear you in their hands,
— Your foot will not stumble on a stone.

With one heart . . . *(As Tuesday Evening)*

118

Collect for the week

The Lord be with you, — And also with you.
Let us pray to the Lord: *(silence, then the collect)* — Amen.

Free Prayer

General Collect

O God, your mercy is for every creature; we pray for all our sisters and brothers, commending to you those who are at present dying. To each and to all of us grant a share in the joy of the saints in light, through Jesus Christ, your Son, our Lord, — Amen.

Blessing

The seven words from our Lord on the Cross:
Father, forgive them. They do not know what they are doing.
I tell you, today you will be with me in Paradise.
Mother, here is your son—And here is your mother.
My God, my God, why have you abandoned me?
I am thirsty.
It is finished.
Father, into your hands I give my spirit.
— Truly, this man was the Son of God.

Let us bless the Lord,
— We give our thanks to God.

May the God of all grace, who has called us to his eternal glory in Christ, after we have suffered for a while, make us perfect, confirm and strengthen us; to him be the power for ever and ever.
— Amen.

SATURDAY MORNING

Introduction

Return to the Lord, he has pity on you,
— To God, he is all forgiveness.

I remember all you have done,
— I ponder on the work of your hands;
I hold out my hands to you,
— My soul is parched land, thirsting for you.

Come quickly, answer me, Lord!
— I am faint and breathless;
If you hide much longer,
— I shall fall among the dead.

Let morning bring proof of your love,
— For I count on you.
Show me the way I should take,
— For to you I lift my soul.

To him who reigns from the throne, and to the Lamb,
— Praise and honour, glory and power for ever and ever.
Amen.

Psalm — Old Testament

Responses: *As Wednesday Morning*

Gospel — Silence

Intercession: *As Weanesday Morning*

Collect for the week

The Lord be with you, — And also with you.
Let us pray to the Lord: *(silence, then the collect)* — Amen.

Free Prayer

General Collect

O God, you alone know those who love you; we pray you to guide in the ways of eternal life all those entrusted to our prayers, through Jesus Christ, our Lord,   — Amen.

The Lord's Prayer

O Christ, remember us in your Kingdom,
— Lord, teach us to pray: Our Father . . .

Blessing

Let us bless the Lord,
— We give our thanks to God.

May the peace of God, which surpasses all understanding, keep our hearts and our minds in Christ Jesus.
— Amen.

SATURDAY EVENING

Introduction

Return to the Lord, your God,
— For he is tenderness and compassion.

Teach me to do your will,
— For you are my God;
May your good Spirit guide me,
— Into plain paths.

For your Name's sake, O Lord,
— May I live in your justice;
Draw my life from oppression,
— For I am your servant.

Worthy is the Lamb that was slain
to receive power and riches and wisdom,
— Strength, honour, glory and praise. Amen.

Psalm — Epistle

Responses: *As Wednesday Evening*

Silence — Hymn

Intercession

The angels will bear you in their hands,
— Your foot will not stumble on a stone.

Lord have mercy,
— Christ have mercy,

Lord have mercy,
— Christ hear us.

God the Father in heaven,
— Mercy for us!

122

God the Son, Redeemer of the world,
— Mercy for us!

God the Holy Spirit,
— Mercy for us!

God, one God, thrice holy,
— Mercy for us!

O Crucified Jesus, Son of the Father, conceived by the Holy Spirit, born of the Virgin Mary, eternal Word of God:
— We worship you!

O Crucified Jesus, holy temple of God, dwelling-place of the Most High, door of heaven, burning flame of charity:
— We worship you!

O Crucified Jesus, sanctuary of justice and love, full of kindness, source of all faithfulness:
— We worship you!

O Crucified Jesus, King and Master of every heart, in you are all the treasures of wisdom and knowledge, in you dwells all the fulness of godhead, in you the Father finds his joy:
— We worship you!

Lamb of God, you take away the sin of the world,
— Lord forgive!

Lamb of God, you take away the sin of the world,
— Lord hear us!

Lamb of God, you take away the sin of the world,
— Lord have mercy on us!

Jesus, gentle and humble of heart,
— Give us hearts like yours.

Collect for the week

The Lord be with you, — And also with you.
Let us pray to the Lord: *(silence, then the collect)* — Amen.

Free Prayer

General Collect

O Christ, the only Son of God, Redeemer of the world, free
us from all evil and keep us in all things alert and faithful,
until the coming of your Kingdom, where there is no more
sorrow, for you live and reign now and for ever,   — Amen.

Blessing

After his spirit has been tested,
— The Servant will see light and be comforted;
By his sufferings he will justify thousands,
— Taking their faults upon himself.

Let us bless the Lord,
— We give our thanks to God.

May almighty God bless us,
the Father, the Son and the Holy Spirit.
— Amen.

Introduction to the Gospel

(Hymn or Psalm)
For the . . . Sunday in Lent, the Gospel according to . . .

Song of the Firstborn

He is the Image of the unseen God,
— The Firstborn of all creation.
For in him all things were made,
— In heaven and on the earth.

All was created through him and for him,
— He was before all things, and everything exists in him;
He is also the Head of his Body, the Church,
— He is the Beginning, the Firstborn from the dead.

God meant all his fulness to live in him,
— And reconciled through him all creation to himself,
Everything on earth and everything in the heavens,
— All gathered into peace by his death on the Cross.

Holy Week

The liturgy of Holy Week allows us to follow Christ step by step along his way of sacrifice; but it is always dominated at every moment by the expectation of his Easter victory.

Psalms and responses are the very expression of the Saviour's suffering, and the Church, in her use of them, joins with the prayers offered by Christ to his Father in the course of his Passion. Thus the Church is united with her crucified Lord, and utters the words of his agony. And she blends into the prayer of Christ all the suffering in the world for which Jesus gave his life.

PALM SATURDAY EVENING AND
PALM SUNDAY MORNING

Introduction

Praise to him who is coming in the name of the Lord!
— Hosanna in highest heaven!

Rejoice with heart and soul, daughter of Zion!
— Shout aloud with joy, daughter of Jerusalem!
See, your King is coming to you,
— He is just, he is victorious.
Humble, riding on an ass,
— He will proclaim peace to the nations.

Gates, raise your arches! Rise, eternal doors!
— Let the King of glory come in!

Psalm 147 (evening) 23 (morning)

Epistle (evening: Phil. 2.5-11)

Short Reading (morning)

Living life as a man, Jesus humbled himself in complete
obedience, accepting even death, and death on a cross.

Responses

With palms in their hands, they went singing to welcome the
Lord and cried out in joy:
Hosanna! Praise to the King coming for us in the name of the
Lord!
— With palms in their hands . . .

Close your ranks and move forward, branches in hand, up to
the altar.
— Hosanna! Praise . . .

Open the gates of goodness: I will go in, I will give thanks.
— Hosanna! Praise . . .

This is the gate of the Lord: the good shall enter in.
— Hosanna! Praise . . .

Praise for the Kingdom to come, from David our father!
— With palms in their hands . . .

Silence — Hymn

Praise

The hour is come for the Son of Man to be glorified.
— When I am raised from the earth I will draw all men to
myself.

Today, the Holy Spirit has brought us together, and, looking
to the cross of Christ, we all say: Glory, praise and honour to
you, O Jesus, our King and our Redeemer, to whom the
people sang in love: Hosanna! Praise to the King who is
coming!
— Hosanna! Praise to the King who is coming!

You are the King of Israel and the Son of David. You have
come in the name of the Lord, our King most blessed.
— Hosanna! praise to the King who is coming!

All the company of angels sing in exultation, and mortals with
the whole of creation join in your praise.
— Hosanna! . . .

The Hebrew people went out with palms to meet you, we
meet you now with our prayers, our vows and our praises.
— Hosanna! . . .

You were moving on to your Passion when they brought you
their praises, you are reigning now in glory as we express our
joy.
— Hosanna! . . .

You enjoyed their celebrations, accept ours too with delight,
O King full of goodness and mercy. You rejoice in our love.
— Hosanna! . . .

Collect

The Lord be with you, — And also with you.
Let us pray to the Lord: *(silence).*

Lord God of love, increase our faith. You poured blessings on
Noah as he left the ark, and on Moses when he set out from
Egypt with the children of Israel. May we leave our slavery
behind us and go forward to meet Christ with palms in our
hands, for he will lead us into your eternal joy.   — Amen.

Free Prayer

Collect

Almighty and eternal God, you raise up and save us through
the Passion of Christ; as we celebrate this wonder, finish in us
the work you have begun and plant new zeal in our hearts,
through Jesus Christ, your Son, our Lord.   — Amen.

Blessing

Let us bless the Lord,
— We give our thanks to God.

May God almighty bless us,
the Father, the Son and the Holy Spirit.
— Amen.

Gospel (Saturday evening)

Hosanna to the Son of David! Praise to him who is coming in
the name of the Lord!
— Hosanna . . .

129

Clap your hands, all you nations,
raise to the Lord pæans of joy;
For the Lord, the Highest, is the great King
over all the earth.
We stand in awe before him.
— Hosanna . . .

For Palm Sunday, Gospel according to Saint Matthew (21.1-9).

PALM SUNDAY EVENING

Introduction

Lord, do not stay away, my agony is near,
— O my strength, come quickly, help me!

My God, my God, why have you abandoned me!
— My groaning does nothing to save me!
I call all day, and you give no heed,
— I call all night, I am never silent!

Lord, my Lord, do not stay away,
— O my strength, come quickly, help me.
Save my soul from the sword,
— My life from the jaws of the hounds.

The Lord has never despised,
— Nor disdained the despair of the poor,
Never from them has he hidden,
— Answering whenever they called.

Lord my God, look down and answer me,
— Give light to my eyes, or they will close in death.

Psalm 85

The Reading of the Passion

(At every reading of the Passion, there can be three readers: the text of the Evangelist, the words of Christ, the other persons. The readings can be interrupted by the singing of verses from hymns of the Passion.)
The Passion of our Lord Jesus Christ, told by Saint Matthew (26.30-75) . . .

Responses

Lord, do not stay away, my agony is near,
+ O my strength, come quickly, help me!
— Lord . . .

All who see me laugh me to scorn,
shaking their heads and sneering.
— O my strength, come quickly, help me!

They pierce my hands and my feet,
they leave me lying for dead.
— O my strength . . .

They share my clothing among them,
casting lots for my cloak.
— O my strength . . .

But I shall live for Him, and my people shall praise Him;
proclaiming the Lord for ages to come.
— Lord, do not stay away . . .

Silence — Hymn

Intercession

The hour has come for the Son of Man to be glorified:
— Raised up from the earth, I will draw all men to myself.

Lord of all the worlds, come and revive us,
— Smile upon us and we shall be saved.

Rise Lord, come to our aid,
— Set us free for your love's sake.

O Lord, hear our prayer,
— Let our cry come before you.

Collect

The Lord be with you, — And also with you.
Let us pray to the Lord: *(silence)*

Lord, with all our hearts we love you; the death of your Son
gives us the sure hope of freedom, bring us then by his rising
again to that goal promised by our victorious King, Jesus
Christ your Son, our Saviour.   — Amen.

132

Free Prayer

Collect

Almighty and eternal God, you raise us up and save us through the Passion of your Christ. As we celebrate this wonder, finish in us the work you have begun, and plant new zeal in our hearts through Jesus Christ, your Son, our Lord. — Amen.

Blessing

Let us bless the Lord,
— We give our thanks to God.

May the Lord bless us, the Maker of heaven and earth.
— Amen.

MONDAY, TUESDAY AND WEDNESDAY
IN HOLY WEEK: MORNINGS

Introduction

Lord, do not stay away, my agony is near,
— O my strength, come quickly, help me!

Like a tree he grew in our sight,
— From a root in the arid earth.
We could see no beauty, no majesty,
— No grace to delight our eyes.

He was despised and rejected by men,
— A Man of Sorrows, accustomed to pain,
A sight to avert the eyes,
— Despised and of no account.

or:

Our fathers hoped in you,
— They hoped and you delivered them;
When they called on you, they escaped,
— Never did they hope in vain.

Lord my God, look down and answer me,
— Give light to my eyes, or they will close in death.

Psalm 34, v. 1–18 (*Monday*); 68, v. 15–37 (*Tuesday*); 139 (*Wednesday*).

Old Testament

Responses

Monday:
The spirit is willing, but the flesh is weak.
— The spirit . . .

On the Mount of Olives, Jesus prayed his Father:
Father, if it is possible, O let this Cup pass me by!
— The spirit . . .

134

Stay awake, pray to avoid temptation.
— The spirit . . .

Tuesday:
Jesus, remember me when you come into your Kingdom.
— Jesus, remember . . .

The veil of the Temple was rent, the earth began to quake, and the robber said:
— Jesus, remember . . .

The rocks split, the graves opened and the bodies of many saints rose again:
— Jesus, remember . . .

Wednesday:
So by his wounds we are all saved and healed.
— So by his wounds . . .

We saw him. He had no beauty, no majesty; he was bearing our sins; for us he suffered, pierced through by our faults.
— So by his wounds . . .

It was our distress that he bore, our pains were pressing him down.
— So by his wounds . . .

The Reading of the Passion

Monday: Matt. 27 1–56; *Tuesday:* Mark 15 1–41; *Wednesday:* Luke 23 13–49.

Responses

Monday:
My heart is breaking with grief, stay with me and watch with me.
— My heart is breaking . . .

Anguish and dismay came over him,
he fell prostrate on the ground, and he prayed:
— My heart is breaking . . .

And now the hour has come. The Son of Man is betrayed
into the hands of sinful men.
— My heart is breaking . . .

Tuesday:
You have crucified me and set free Barabbas.
— You have crucified me . . .

O vineyard that I have loved, that I planted with my own
hands, how have you yielded such bitter fruit?
— You have crucified me . . .

I built a wall round you, I lifted out your stones.
And I built the watch-tower.
— You have crucified me . . .

Wednesday:
All you passing by along the road, look and see if any grief
can be compared with mine.
— All you passing by . . .

My God, my God, why have you abandoned me?
— All you passing by . . .

Father, into your hands I give my spirit.
— All you passing by . . .

Silence — Intercession

Deliver me from my enemies, my God,
— Protect me against my attackers.

Lamb of God, you take away the sin of the world, have mercy
on us:
— Strengthen us, Lord.

Lamb of God, you take away the sin of the world, receive our prayer:
— Strengthen us, Lord.

Lamb of God, you take away the sin of the world, grant us your peace:
— Strengthen us, Lord.

By your human birth and your dire poverty, by your fastings and your temptations, by your distress and anguish of soul, and by all your pain:
— Strengthen us, Lord.

By your agony, by your bonds and your insults, by your scourging and your crown of thorns, and by your nailing to the cross:
— Strengthen us, Lord.

By your wounds and your bitter death, by your descent from the cross and your resting in the grave:
— Strengthen us, Lord.

By your resurrection and your last days on earth, by your ascension and your reigning in power, by your continual intercession, and by your return in glory:
— Strengthen us, Lord.

May your willing acceptance of death reveal the mystery of your love for us; may your tears soothe our pains and our griefs; may your broken body and your blood poured forth be the food of our eternal life.
— Strengthen us, Lord.

Collect

The Lord be with you, — And also with you.
Let us pray to the Lord: *(silence)*

Almighty God, we pray you by the Passion of your beloved Son to help us in all our trials, and to be the strength for our human weakness, through Christ who lives and reigns for ever,   — Amen.

Free Prayer

Collect (as on Palm Sunday evening)

The Lord's Prayer

O Christ, remember us in your Kingdom,
— Lord, teach us to pray: Our Father . . .

Blessing

Let us bless the Lord,
— We give our thanks to God.

May our Lord Jesus Christ himself, and God our Father who has loved us, and given us by his grace eternal consolation and joyful hope, comfort our hearts and strengthen them in every good word and work.
— Amen.

MONDAY, TUESDAY AND WEDNESDAY
IN HOLY WEEK: EVENINGS

Introduction

Lord, do not stay away, my agony is near,
— O my strength, come quickly, help me!

Ours were the sufferings he bore,
— And ours the torments he endured.
While we thought he was punished,
— Struck down by God and disgraced.

He was pierced for our sins,
— Bruised for no fault but ours.
His punishment has won our peace,
— And by his wounds we are whole.

Lord my God, look down and answer me,
— Give light to my eyes, or they will close in death.

Psalm 66 (*Monday*); 101 (*Tuesday*); 140 (*Wednesday*).

Old Testament

Responses (as on the mornings)

The Reading of the Passion
Monday: Mark 14 26–72; *Tuesday:* Luke 22 39–23 12;
Wednesday: ad libitum

Responses (as on the mornings)

Silence — Hymn

Intercession
Keep me Lord from the hands of the godless,
— Defend me from the man of violence.

139

Let us think on Jesus the Lord: instead of the joy meant for him, he endured the cross, ignoring its disgrace:
— We worship you Lord upon the Cross.

O Jesus Christ, the King of glory, born in humility to confound the proud and to raise the humble, you became the poor workman of Nazareth to teach us true wealth.
— We worship you Lord upon the Cross.

You went among us, doing good, proclaiming the good news to the poor and freedom to prisoners.
— We worship you . . .

You came to loose the chains of every slavery, friend of the humble, bread of hungry souls, healer of the sick.
— We worship you . . .

Jesus, pattern of patience and goodness, prophet of the Kingdom of God, Master, gentle and humble of heart, forgiving all who loved much, and calling the weary and the burdened.
— We worship you . . .

Jesus, you came into the world to serve and to lay down your life, you had nowhere to lay your head, you were betrayed for money, dragged before Pilate and nailed to the Cross.
— We worship you . . .

Jesus, Lord of all the worlds by your resurrection from the dead, alive for ever to intercede with your Father and ours.
— We worship you . . .

Collect (as mornings)

Free Prayer

Collect

O God, by the blood of your beloved Son, poured forth on the Cross, you restored our peace and made us the inheritors of your Kingdom; grant us to find in you surpassing peace and continually to rejoice in the communion of all your saints, through Jesus Christ our Lord, — Amen.

Blessing

Let us bless the Lord,
— We give our thanks to God.

May the God of all grace, who has called us to his eternal glory in Christ, after we have suffered for a while, make us perfect, confirm and strengthen us; to him be the power for ever and ever.
— Amen.

Psalm 53

Lamentations

I burn with zeal for your house,
— The taunting of your enemies wounds me.

The lamentations of the prophet over the persecuted People
of God gather the sufferings of all into the communion of the
Crucified Christ. Let us ask his help for all who are now
suffering in the world.

Reading from the Lamentations of Jeremiah:
— Jerusalem, Jerusalem, return to the Lord your God.

Lam. 2 11–13
— Jerusalem . . .

Lam. 2 14–16
— Jerusalem . . .

Lam. 2 17–19
— Jerusalem . . .

Responses

The spirit is willing, but the flesh is weak.
— The spirit . . .

On the Mount of Olives, Jesus prayed his Father:
Father, if it is possible, O let this Cup pass me by!
— The spirit . . .

Stay awake, pray to avoid temptation.
— The spirit . . .

Silence

Psalm 54 v. 1–19

Old Testament

You have seized me by my right hand, you will lead me with your counsel.
— Then you will take me into glory.

Reading from the book Deuteronomy (*Deut.* 16 1–3).

Responses

My heart is breaking with grief, stay with me and watch with me.
— My heart is breaking . . .

Anguish and dismay came over him,
he fell prostrate on the ground, and he prayed:
— My heart is breaking . . .

And now the hour has come. The son of Man is betrayed into the hands of sinful men.
— My heart is breaking . . .

Silence

Psalm 55

Gospel

In the day of distress I seek the Lord,
— At night, I hold out my hand to him.
(*Either Matt.* 26 17–29, *or Mark* 14 12–25, *or Luke* 22 1–13)

Responses

So by his wounds we are all saved and healed.
— So by his wounds . . .

143

We saw him. He had no beauty, no majesty; he was bearing our sins; for us he suffered, pierced through by our faults.
— So by his wounds . . .

It was our distress that he bore, our pains were pressing him down.
— So by his wounds . . .

Silence

Christ became obedient unto death for us,
— Christ became obedient . . .
Our Father . . .

Collect

Lord, we pray you, look upon your family for whom our Lord Jesus Christ was willing to undergo the torture of the Cross. Now he reigns with you and the Holy Spirit for ever, — Amen.

Psalm 146

Antiphon:

You have restored us Lord, by your power, and by the sacred meal you have given us.

Gospel

When harshly treated, he suffered humbly, he uttered never a word,
— Like a sheep, dumb before the shearers.

From the Gospel according to Saint Luke: (*Luke* 22 14–23)

Responses

My heart is breaking . . . *(as morning)*

Silence — Intercession (if suitable)

Let us implore our Redeemer, who suffered his Passion, was buried and rose again from the dead, saying: O Christ, we adore you.
— O Christ, we adore you.

Lord our Master, for us you became obedient unto death, teach us to do your Father's will.
— O Christ . . .

Lord our Life, by dying on the Cross you have conquered death and the powers of darkness, enable us to share in your death and in your resurrection into glory.
— O Christ . . .

Lord our Strength, you were despised by men, humiliated as a condemned criminal, teach us true humility.
— O Christ . . .

Lord our Salvation, you gave your life for love of your brothers, teach us to love one another with that same love.
— O Christ . . .

Lord our Lord, with hands outstretched on the Cross, you draw all to yourself, gather into your Kingdom all the scattered children of God.
— O Christ . . .

Christ became obedient unto death for us.
— Christ became obedient . . .

Collect (as morning)

(The Common Prayer for the evening of Maundy Thursday is the Eucharist of the Last Supper, in which the Church celebrates the last meal of Christ with his disciples, when he washed their feet, instituted the Sacrament of his Body and Blood, and left them the New Commandment to love one another.)

Psalm 2

Lamentations

My strength is spent, my heart is throbbing,
— The very light has gone from my eyes.

The lamentations of the prophet . . . *(as on Maundy Thursday Morning)*
— Jerusalem, Jerusalem, return to the Lord your God.

Lam. 3 1–9
— Jerusalem . . .

Lam. 3 10–18
— Jerusalem . . .

Lam. 3 19–26
— Jerusalem . . .

Responses

All you passing by along the road, look and see
if any grief can be compared with mine.
— All you passing by . . .

My God, my God, why have you abandoned me?
— All you passing by . . .

Father, into your hands I give my spirit.
— All you passing by . . .

Silence

Psalm 93 v. 12–22

Reading

False witnesses have risen against me,
— Breathing out violence.
From the Letter to the Hebrews: (*Heb.* 9 11–15).

Responses

Jesus, remember me when you come into your Kingdom.
— Jesus, remember . . .

The veil of the temple was rent, the earth began to quake,
and the robber said:
— Jesus, remember . . .

The rocks split, the graves opened and the bodies of many
saints rose again.
— Jesus, remember . . .

Silence

Psalm 142

Gospel

They besiege me with venomous words,
— They attack me for no reason.
From the Gospel according to Saint John: (*John* 18 1–11).

Responses

You have crucified me and set free Barabbas.
— You have crucified me . . .

O vineyard that I have loved, that I planted with my own
hands, how have you yielded such bitter fruit?
— You have crucified me . . .

I built a wall round you, I lifted out your stones,
And I built the watch-tower.
— You have crucified me . . .

148

Silence

Christ became obedient unto death for us, obedient unto death upon a Cross.
— Christ became obedient . . .
Our Father . . .

Collect

Lord, we pray you, look upon your family for whom our Lord Jesus Christ was willing to undergo the torture of the Cross. Now he reigns with you and the Holy Spirit for ever,
— Amen.

Psalm 21

Reading

He makes me dwell in darkness,
— Like those who are sunk in death.

They crucified him and shared out his clothes, casting lots for each garment; it was the third hour when they crucified him. At the sixth hour, about midday, darkness fell over the whole country until the ninth hour.

Responses

All you passing by along the road, look and see
if any grief can be compared with mine.
— All you passing by . . .

My God, my God, why have you abandoned me?
— All you passing by . . .

Father, into your hands I give my spirit.
— All you passing by . . .

Silence

Intercession (as on Maundy Thursday noon)

Collect

Christ became obedient unto death for us, obedient unto death upon a Cross.
— Christ became . . .

Lord we pray you, look upon your family for whom our Lord Jesus Christ was willing to undergo the torture of the Cross. Now he reigns with you and the Holy Spirit for ever,
— Amen.

CELEBRATION OF THE CROSS

(This form of celebration is shorter than the full Liturgy of the Church; it is intended to furnish a continuity with the preceding and following celebrations of Holy Week.)

Introduction

O my people, what have I done to you? How have I grieved you?
Answer me! — Kyrie eleison!

or, in place of Kyrie eleison:
God, holy; God, strong and holy;
God, holy and immortal: have pity on us.

I freed you from slavery, I engulfed your Enemy:
you handed me over, you jeered at me!
— O my people . . . — Kyrie eleison!

I opened the sea before you:
you opened my side with your spear!
— O my people . . . — Kyrie eleison!

I moved before you in the pillar of cloud:
you led me to Pilate!
— O my people . . . — Kyrie eleison!

I watched over you in the desert and fed you with manna:
you struck me and scourged me!
— O my people . . . — Kyrie eleison!

I gave you from the rock living waters of salvation:
you gave me gall to drink, you quenched my thirst with vinegar!
— O my people . . . — Kyrie eleison!

I struck down kings for you:
you struck me with a reed!
— O my people . . . — Kyrie eleison!

I put the sceptre into your hand, I made you a royal people:
you crowned me with the crown of thorns!
— O my people . . . — Kyrie eleison!

I made you great by my boundless power:
you hanged me on the gallows of the Cross!
— O my people . . . — Kyrie eleison!

Song of the Redeemer

We worship you Lord upon the Cross,
and your Resurrection in power we proclaim and glorify.
— We worship you . . .

For by the Cross joy has broken forth for all that exists.
— We worship you . . .

God be gracious to us and bless us
— And smile down upon us;
The world will acknowledge your ways,
— All nations your power to save.

— We worship you Lord . . .

Let the people rejoice and sing,
— For you judge the world justly;
You judge the nations with equity,
— You govern the nations on the earth.

— We worship you . . .

The earth has yielded her harvest,
— God, our God has blessed us.
Lord, bless us! May you be worshipped
— To all the ends of the earth.

— We worship you . . .

Collect

Remember, Lord, your kindness towards us; ever sanctify and protect your children, for whom Christ Jesus our Lord shed his blood upon the Cross and so accomplished the paschal mystery; he lives and reigns with you, Father, and the Holy Spirit, now and for ever, — Amen.

Old Testament

(Isaiah 53 10–12)

Responses

All you passing by along the road, look and see
if any grief can be compared with mine.
— All you passing by . . .

My God, my God, why have you abandoned me?
— All you passing by . . .

Father, into your hands I give my spirit.
— All you passing by . . .

Epistle

(Hebrews 4 14–16; 5 7–9)

Responses

Jesus, remember me when you come into your Kingdom.
— Jesus, remember . . .

The veil of the temple was rent, the earth began to quake,
and the robber said:
— Jesus, remember . . .

The rocks split, the graves opened
and the bodies of many saints rose again.
— Jesus, remember . . .

153

The Reading of the Passion

(John 18 12–19 37)

Responses

You have crucified me and set free Barabbas.
— You have crucified me . . .

O vineyard that I have loved, that I planted with my own hands, how have you yielded such bitter fruit?
— You have crucified me . . .

I built a wall round you, I lifted out your stones,
And I built the watchtower.
— You have crucified me . . .

The Great Intercession

(The exact form of this intercession may vary according to traditions and circumstances: biddings followed by collects, free prayers etc. Themes should include: the whole Church throughout the world; those exercising a ministry in the Church; people now preparing to become part of the People of God; the unity of all Christians; Jews, Moslems, those of other faiths; people unable to believe; all who exercise power in the world; all who suffer . . .)

Blessing

We worship you Lord upon the Cross,
and your Resurrection in power we proclaim and glorify.
— We worship you . . .

For by the Cross joy has broken forth for all that exists.
— We worship you . . .

Almighty Father, pour out the fulness of blessings on your People; we have celebrated the dying of your Son and look towards his Resurrection from the dead; give us pardon and peace, increase our faith and be our eternal salvation through Jesus Christ our Lord.
— Amen.

GOOD FRIDAY: EVENING

Introduction

O my people, what have I done to you? How have I grieved you?
Answer me! — Kyrie eleison!

I freed you from slavery, I engulfed your Enemy:
you handed me over, you jeered at me!
— O my people . . . — Kyrie eleison!

I opened the sea before you:
you opened my side with your spear!
— O my people . . . — Kyrie eleison!

I moved before you in the pillar of cloud:
you led me to Pilate!
— O my people . . . — Kyrie eleison!

I watched over you in the desert and fed you with manna:
you struck me and scourged me!
— O my people . . . — Kyrie eleison!

Psalms

Ps. 1; antiphon:
The tree of life is your Cross, O Lord!

Ps. 4; antiphon:
Soon I will lie down and fall peacefully asleep.

Ps. 114; antiphon:
I will walk in God's presence in the land of the living.

Gospel

(*either:* John 19 38–42; *or* Mark 15 42–47; *or* Luke 23 50–56)

Responses

My life is on the brink of hell.
— My life ...

They think I have gone down to the grave
like a man dead and gone.
— My life ...

I am shut out from among the living,
like a body lying in the tomb.
— My life ...

Silence — Hymn

Song of the Burial

Joseph of Arimathea took your Body down from the Cross;
he wrapped it in a shroud with spices;
reverently he laid it in a new tomb.

Collect

O God, it is your will that we should be baptised into the death
of your Son our Saviour; give us true repentance that we may
pass with him through the grave and gate of death, and be
reborn to new life in joy, through him who died, was buried
and who rose for us, Jesus our Lord.
— Amen.

HOLY SATURDAY: MORNING

Introduction

O my people what have I done to you? How have I grieved you?
Answer me! — Kyrie eleison!

I gave you from the rock living waters of salvation:
you gave me gall to drink, you quenched my thirst with vinegar!
— O my people ... — Kyrie eleison!

I struck down kings for you:
you struck me with a reed!
— O my people ... — Kyrie eleison!

I put the sceptre into your hand, I made you a royal people:
you crowned me with the crown of thorns!
— O my people ... — Kyrie eleison!

I made you great by my boundless power:
you hanged me on the gallows of the Cross!
— O my people ... — Kyrie eleison!

Psalm 87

Antiphon:

You have sent me to the bottom of the Pit,
into the darkest depths of the abyss.

Lamentations

I believe, I shall see the goodness of God in the land of the Living.
— Hope in God, take heart and be of good courage!
The lamentations of the prophet ... *(as on Maundy Thursday morning)*

— Jerusalem, Jerusalem, return to the Lord your God.

Lam. 3 27–33
— Jerusalem . . .

Lam. 3 46–51
— Jerusalem . . .

Lam. 3 52–58
— Jerusalem . . .

Responses

My life on the brink of hell.
— My life . . .

They think I have gone down to the grave,
like a man dead and gone.
— My life . . .

I am shut out from among the living,
like a body lying in the tomb.
— My life . . .

Silence

Psalm 29

Antiphon:

Lord, you have brought up my soul from hell, you have
revived me.

Epistle

Lord, have pity on me, raise me up,
— And I will know that you are my friend.

From the first Letter of Peter (1 *Pet.* 3 18–22).

Responses

Because of evil, the good man is taken,
to enter into peace.
— Because of evil . . .

The good man perishes and not a soul gives heed.
— Because of evil . . .

The man of faith is taken away and no one cares.
— Because of evil . . .

Silence

Psalm 15

Antiphon:
My heart exults and my soul rejoices, my body will rest secure.

Gospel

God, come to my rescue,
— Lord, support and save me.
From the Gospel according to St Matthew: (*Matt.* 27 57–66)

Responses

Arise and call in the night,
through the early, silent watches.
— Arise . . .

Pour out your heart like water before the Lord.
— Arise . . .

And lift up your hands to him.
— Arise . . .

Silence — Anthem

Christ became obedient unto death for us,
obedient unto death upon a cross.
— Christ became obedient . . .

And God has exalted him,
giving him the Name above every name.
— Christ became obedient . . .

Our Father . . .

Collect

O God, it is your will that we should be baptised into the death of your Son our Saviour; give us true repentance that we may pass with him through the grave and gate of death, and be reborn to new life in joy, through him who died, was buried and who rose for us, Jesus our Lord.

— Amen.

HOLY SATURDAY: NOON

Introduction *(as Good Friday evening, if needed)*

Psalm 141

Verse

You will not leave my soul in hell,
— Nor permit your friend to see corruption.

We have been buried with Christ by our baptism.

Responses

Because of evil, the good man is taken,
to enter into peace.
— Because of evil . . .

The good man perishes and not a soul gives heed.
— Because of evil . . .

The man of faith is taken away and no one cares.
— Because of evil . . .

Silence

Intercession *(if needed)*

Let us implore our Redeemer who suffered his Passion, was
buried and rose again from the dead, saying: O Christ, we
adore you.
— O Christ, we adore you.

O Saviour Christ, your grief-stricken Mother was present at
your Cross and burial: enable us to share in your Passion at
our times of testing.
— O Christ, we adore you.

O Lord Christ, like the seed of wheat fallen into the ground, you have borne the fruit of the life of God: may we die to sin and live for God.

— O Christ, we adore you.

O Christ the New Adam, you descended into the kingdom of the dead to set the good free from captivity: may your voice be heard by all who have died in sin, that they may live.

— O Christ, we adore you.

O Christ Son of the living God, through baptism we have been buried with you in death: make us partners in your resurrection, that we may walk in newness of life.

— O Christ, we adore you.

Anthem

Christ became obedient unto death for us,
obedient unto death upon a Cross.
— Christ . . .

And God has exalted him,
giving him the Name above every name.
— Christ . . .

Collect (as morning)

HOLY SATURDAY: EVENING

Introduction *(as Holy Saturday morning, if needed)*

Confession and Absolution

Minister: Brother, give us the blessing of the Lord:

Officiant: May the almighty Lord grant us a quiet night and a peaceful end.

All: Amen.

Officiant: Let us prepare to celebrate Easter by acknowledging that we are sinners *(silence)*

All: I confess to almighty God, and I acknowledge before you all, that I have sinned in thought, in word and in deed; it was all my fault, my own fault, my own great fault. I ask you all then, in the communion of saints, to pray for me to the Lord our God.

Officiant: May God almighty have mercy on us; may he forgive us our sins and bring us to eternal life.

All: Amen.

Officiant: To all who repent and seek Jesus Christ for their salvation, I declare absolution of their sin, in the name of the Father, the Son and the Holy Spirit.

All: Amen.

Psalm 90

Reading

I know that my Redeemer is alive,
and that he will arise on earth at last;
when I awake, he will set me beside him,
and, in my flesh, I shall see God.
I will see him, he will take my part,
my eyes will look on no stranger.
My heart is fainting within me.

Responses

Arise and call in the night,
through the early, silent watches.
— Arise ...

Pour out your heart like water before the Lord.
— Arise ...

And lift up your hands to him.
— Arise ...

Silence

Intercession *(if needed)*

Let us implore our Redeemer who suffered his Passion, was buried and rose again from the dead, saying: O Christ, we adore you.
— O Christ, we adore you.

Lord Jesus, from your side pierced by the spear poured water and blood, in token of the birth of your Church: by your death, your burial and your resurrection, give life to your People.
— O Christ ...

Lord Jesus, you remembered those who had forgotten the promise of your resurrection: remember too those who live without hope, knowing nothing of the resurrection.
— O Christ ...

Lamb of God, our Passover, you were sacrificed for all: draw all people to yourself.
— O Christ ...

God of the universe, whom the whole world cannot contain, you were willing to be enclosed in the tomb: preserve all from eternal death and give us glorious immortality.
— O Christ ...

O Christ, Son of the living God, you descended into the dwelling of the dead, have pity on all who like yourself have known death and the grave: and let us all share the glory of your resurrection.

— O Christ . . .

Song of Simeon

Save us, Lord, when we are awake;
guard us, Lord, when we are asleep;
awake we will watch with Christ,
and asleep we will rest in peace.

Now, Lord, give your servant his discharge,
— In peace, according to your promise.
For my eyes have seen your own Christ,
— Prepared by you for the nations.

A light to lighten all mankind,
— The glory of Israel your People.
Glory to Father, to Son and Holy Spirit
— For ever and ever. Amen.

Save us, Lord . . .

Collect

The Lord be with you,—And also with you.
Let us pray in peace: *(silence)*.

Almighty God, grant to us, who are about to celebrate Christ's resurrection, such grace, that at the last we may come to the glory of a resurrection like his, in the eternal Kingdom of Jesus Christ, your Son, our Lord, who now lives, and reigns, with you, O Father, and with you, O Holy Spirit, God and Saviour for ever and ever.　　　　　　　　　　— Amen.

Blessing

Let us bless the Lord,
— We give our thanks to God.

May the almighty and merciful Lord, Father, Son and Holy Spirit, bless us and keep us.
— Amen.

Easter

The celebration of the Resurrection in the early hours of Easter Day, through the great Easter Vigil, is the climax of the liturgy. No form of the Vigil liturgies is given here, since they exist in official forms elsewhere.

The Vigil marks the beginning of a week of paschal festival, and this Easter Week is the joyful counterpart of the celebration of the Passion during Holy Week.

The weeks following, still part of the paschal festival, lead up to the celebration of Christ's Entry into his Glory in the Ascension. These forty days between Easter and the Ascension are in contrast to the forty days of Lent.

The climax of all is Pentecost, the festival of the Holy Spirit sent by the Father into the Church. A new presence of God, and a new relationship between us and the Father, a share in the life of the Risen Christ, and the beginning of the fulfilment of all the promises: such is the reality the liturgy celebrates particularly at Pentecost and more generally in every day of the year, in Word and Sacraments, the reality of the presence of Christ among us.

EASTER WEEK: MORNING

Introduction

Alleluia, Christ is risen, Alleluia!
— He really is risen, Alleluia, alleluia!

The stone has been rolled away, Alleluia!
— From the mouth of the tomb, Alleluia, alleluia!
He is not among the dead any more, Alleluia!
— The Living One is risen again, Alleluia, alleluia!
He has conquered by the Cross, Alleluia!
— He has come out of the tomb, Alleluia, alleluia!

Alleluia, our hope is in him, Alleluia!
— He will take us into glory, Alleluia, alleluia!

Psalm — Old Testament

Responses

I am risen again, alleluia!
+ Once again I am close beside you, alleluia!
— I am risen ...

The right hand of the Lord has done wonders,
his right hand has raised me up;
— Once again I am close beside you, alleluia!

No, I shall not die, I shall live.
I shall proclaim what God has done.
— Once again ...

The stone which the builders had rejected
has now become the corner-stone.
— Once again ...

This is the work of God,
and wonderful in our eyes.
— Once again ...

Glory to the Father, and the Son and the Holy Spirit.
— I am risen again . . .

Gospel — Silence

Praise

To the Paschal Victim, let us offer the sacrifice of praise:
— Glory! Lord of Life!

The Lamb has ransomed the flock; the innocent Christ has reconciled sinners to the Father.
— Glory! Lord of Life!

Death and life contended in tremendous strife; the Lord of Life died, but he is alive and he reigns.
— Glory . . .

The disciples saw the tomb of the living Christ, they saw the glory of his resurrection.
— Glory . . .

They saw his angel witnesses, the linen cloth and the shroud.
— Glory . . .

We know for certain: Christ really is risen from the dead!
— Glory . . .

Victorious King, have mercy on us all!
— Glory! Lord of Life!

Collect for the week

The Lord be with you, — And also with you.
Let us pray to the Lord: *(silence, then the collect)* — Amen.

Free Prayer

General Collect

Almighty God, you brighten this season with the glory of the resurrection. Keep us, your family, in the love of Christ. Renew us in body and soul, that our whole lives may be devoted to your service, through Jesus Christ, your Son, our Lord,
— Amen.

The Lord's Prayer

O Christ, remember us in your Kingdom,
— Lord, teach us to pray: Our Father . . .

Blessing

Let us bless the Lord, alleluia, alleluia,
— We give our thanks to God, alleluia, alleluia!

May the God of peace who raised to life the great Shepherd of the sheep, make us ready to do his will in every thing, through Jesus Christ to whom be glory for ever and ever.
— Amen.

EASTER WEEK: EVENING

Introduction: *as morning, or* Psalm 113.

Psalm — Epistle

Responses

O Christ, Son of the Living God, alleluia, alleluia!
— O Christ . . .

You have risen from the dead,
— Alleluia; alleluia!

Glory to the Father, and the Son and the Holy Spirit.
— O Christ . . .

Silence — Hymn

Intercession

O Christ, in your resurrection, alleluia!
— The heavens and the earth rejoice, alleluia!

O Christ, in your resurrection you have burst the gates of the dwelling of the dead. You have destroyed sin and death. By your victory, we implore you: keep us victorious over sin.
— Hear us, Lord of glory.

O Christ, in your resurrection you have rendered death powerless. You have given us new life. By your victory we implore you: direct our lives as your new creation.
— Hear us . . .

O Christ, in your resurrection you have given life to the dead. You have brought all humanity from death to life. By your victory we implore you: give eternal life to all entrusted to us.
— Hear us . . .

O Christ, in your resurrection you confounded your executioners and your guards, and you gladdened your disciples. By your victory we implore you: give us joy in your service.

Collect for the week

The Lord be with you, — And also with you.
Let us pray to the Lord: *(silence, then the collect)* — Amen.

Free Prayer

General Collect: *as morning*

Blessing

You sleeper, awake,
— Rise from the dead!
Upon you will shine the light,
— Jesus Christ, alleluia!

Let us bless the Lord, alleluia, alleluia!
— We give our thanks to God, alleluia, alleluia!

May the almighty and merciful Lord, Father, Son and Holy Spirit, bless us and keep us.
— Amen.

Song of Moses

(on Saturday, for the proclamation of the Gospel)
O sing to the Lord! He has broken through in power and glory, and risen from the dead, alleluia!
— O sing . . .

The Lord is my strength and him alone I praise;
my life he has restored.
— O sing . . .

You will lead us on up to the mountain,
to your holy dwelling, Lord our God,
where you live and reign evermore and evermore.
— O sing . . .

Gospel *(Easter Sunday evening:* Luke 24 13–35; *on the Saturday after Easter:* John 20 24–31.*)*

Hymn

Christ has risen from the dead,
the first fruits of those who fall asleep.
— Death is conquered by life.

Christ has risen from the dead,
death is swallowed up by Life.
— Where then, death, is your victory?

Christ has risen from the dead,
to the God of salvation let us give thanks evermore,
— Through our Lord Jesus Christ.

MONDAY MORNING

Introduction

Give thanks to the Lord for he is good,
— For his love endures for ever, alleluia!

In my distress I cried to the Lord,
— He heard me and set me free.
The Lord is on my side, no more fears!
— What can man do to me?
God is my help above all other;
— I have conquered the enemy.

or:

I know that my Redeemer is alive,
— And at the last he will rise upon the earth.
When I awake, he will set me by his side,
— And in my flesh, I shall see God.

Glory, worship, wisdom, thanksgiving! Alleluia!
— Adoration, power and strength to our God! Alleluia!

Psalm — Old Testament

Responses

The Lord watches over the faithful,
+ He preserves our souls from death, and he restores our
  life.
— The Lord watches ...

Shout for joy to the Lord,
praise is good when the heart is true.
— He preserves ...

The Word of the Lord is right
and all his works are truth.
— He preserves ...

He cherishes justice and right,
the earth is full of his love.
— He preserves . . .

By his Word the heavens were made,
and by the breath of his mouth their glory.
— He prescrves . . .

Glory to the Father, and the Son and the Holy Spirit.
— The Lord watches . . .

Gospel — Silence

Intercession

I know that my Redeemer is alive, alleluia!
— Alive for ever to intercede, alleluia!

Shed your Spirit on all your servants; grant us humility. May
we be subject one to another in Christian love without
pretence.
— Hear us . . .

For love of the peace we find in your presence, keep us in
peace with everyone; give us strength to bless all who curse
us and to do good to all who hate us.
— Hear us . . .

You are the light and salvation of all the nations. Protect
your servants everywhere in the world; send them the fire of
your Spirit as they bear witness to your Resurrection.
— Hear us . . .

Grant to Christians such generosity that all mankind may see
in you the fulfilment of their hopes, and the whole world be
filled with the knowledge of your glory.
— Hear us . . .

Keep us in communion with the Church made perfect and grant that one day we may all be together at rest from our labours in your Kingdom.
— Hear us . . .

Collect for the week
The Lord be with you . . .

Free Prayer

General Collect
Almighty and eternal God, you have reconciled us to yourself through the death and resurrection of your Son and made an everlasting covenant with us. Give us the grace to live what we profess with our lips, in every moment of our lives, through Jesus Christ, your Son, our Lord,   — Amen.

The Lord's Prayer
O Christ, remember us in your Kingdom,
— Lord, teach us to pray: Our Father . . .

Blessing
Let us bless the Lord, alleluia!
— We give our thanks to God, alleluia!

May the God of hope fill us with all joy and all peace in believing, that we may be overflowing with hope through the power of the Holy Spirit.
— Amen.

MONDAY EVENING

Introduction

Give thanks to the Lord for he is good,
— For his love endures for ever, alleluia!

It is better to shelter in the Lord
— Than to count on human nature;
It is better to shelter in the Lord
— Than to count on the powerful.
They all surrounded me, hemming me in,
— In the Name of the Lord I conquered them.

or:

Our Passover, Christ, is now sacrificed;
— Let us celebrate the feast in purity and truth.
We believe in God who raised him from the dead;
— Betrayed for our faults, and raised to justify.

Lord, give salvation, give victory!
— The Lord our God gives us light, alleluia!

Psalm — Epistle

Responses

The Lord is risen from the grave, alleluia, alleluia!
— The Lord . . .

He who for us hung nailed upon the tree,
— Alleluia, alleluia!

Glory to the Father, and the Son and the Holy Spirit.
— The Lord is risen . . .

Silence — Hymn

Intercession

Stay with us, Lord, alleluia!
— For evening draws on, alleluia!

O Christ, Saviour of the world, to whom all power in heaven and on earth is given, cover with your protection all who are exposed to dangers of soul and of body.
— Hear us, Risen Lord!

Guard from temptation all who are threatened, and give peace in believing to those who are worried and harassed.
— Hear us...

Sustain the courage of the oppressed, of prisoners and those persecuted; reveal your power and deliver them.
— Hear us...

Show yourself to the sick, the weak and the dying, that they may be comforted and strengthened.
— Hear us...

Keep us all in mutual love and in the service of your Kingdom.
— Hear us...

Collect for the week

The Lord be with you...

Free Prayer

General Collect

O God of unchanging power, the design of your eternal love is the good of all mankind. So renew the life of your People that all may see the signs of your new creation appearing in the world today, and give glory to the Source of all hope, Christ Jesus our Risen Lord,   — Amen.

Blessing

You sleeper, awake,
— Rise from the dead!
Upon you will shine the light,
— Jesus Christ, alleluia!

Let us bless the Lord, alleluia!
— We give our thanks to God, alleluia!

May the God of peace sanctify us wholly, keeping us blameless in body, mind and soul for the Coming of our Lord Jesus Christ.
— Amen.

TUESDAY MORNING

Introduction

Give thanks to the Lord for he is good,
— For his love endures for ever, Alleluia!

They strove and strove to bring me down,
— But the Lord came to my help;
My strength and my song is God,
— He was my salvation.
Shouts of joy and victory,
— From the tents of the righteous.

or:

The angel of the Lord descended from the sky,
to roll away the stone.
— Flashing like lightning, and his robe was white as snow;
Do not be afraid; you seek Jesus the Crucified;
— He is here no more, but risen as he said.

Glory, worship, wisdom, thanksgiving Alleluia!
— Adoration, power and strength to our God! Alleluia!

Psalm — Old Testament

Responses

O sing to the Lord with praise;
+ He has restored us to life.
— O sing . . .

Shout for God, all the earth,
sing to the glory of his Name.
— He has restored us to life.

Come and see the works of the Lord,
what great wonders he has done for us.
— He has restored . . .

He changed the sea to hard land,
we crossed the river dry-shod.
— He has restored ...

So let our joy be in him,
sovereign of eternal power.
— He has restored ...

Glory to the Father, and the Son and the Holy Spirit.
— O sing to the Lord ...

Gospel — Silence

Intercession

I know that my Redeemer is alive, Alleluia!
— Alive for ever to intercede, Alleluia!

Lord, we call on you. Once you were dead, but now you live
for ever. Conqueror of sin and death, be among us now.
— Amen!

Come to us in your unconquerable power. Prove to our hearts
the goodness of God.
— Amen!

Come and help our divided world. You alone have power to
regenerate and to reconcile.
— Amen!

Strengthen us in the assurance of final victory. Fortify us in
the hope of your Coming.
— Amen!

Make us faithful witnesses to your resurrection. Make us
instruments of your peace.
— Amen!

O Risen Christ, you will fulfil your promises. Blessed be your
glorious name for ever.
— Amen.

181

Collect for the week

The Lord be with you . . .

Free Prayer

General Collect

O God, you did not permit your Son to know the corruption of the tomb. Grant us to share in his glorious life. Strengthen us by his power, that his work may continue in this world, as we await with confidence and joy his triumphant reign in the world to come, for he is alive for ever and ever,　— Amen.

The Lord's Prayer

O Christ . . .

Blessing

Let us bless the Lord, alleluia!
— We give our thanks to God, alleluia!

May the Lord bless us and keep us; may Christ smile upon us and give us his grace; may he unveil his face to us and bring us his peace.
— Amen.

TUESDAY EVENING

Introduction

Give thanks to the Lord for he is good,
— For his love endures for ever, alleluia!

The right hand of the Lord has done wonders,
— His right hand has raised me up.
No, I shall not die, I shall live,
— And I will proclaim the works of God.
The Lord has chastened me again and again,
— But never delivered me to death.

or:

That day in the evening, Jesus came, and stood among them,
— And said: Peace be with you.
He showed them his hands and his side;
— The disciples were filled with joy when they saw the Lord.

Lord, give salvation, give victory!
— The Lord our God gives us light, alleluia!

Psalm — Epistle

Responses

The Lord really has risen into life, alleluia, alleluia!
— The Lord . . .

And he has appeared to Simon.
— Alleluia, alleluia!

Glory to the Father, and the Son and the Holy Spirit.
— The Lord really has risen . . .

Silence — Hymn

Intercession

Stay with us, Lord, alleluia!
— For evening draws on, alleluia!

Risen Son of God, Source of Life, we implore your kindness for ourselves and for all our brothers and sisters.
— Hear us, Lord of glory.

Enable us to live in your life alone, and to walk as children of light in the joy of your victory.
— Hear us . . .

Increase the faith of your Church, that she may give faithful witness to your resurrection.
— Hear us . . .

Comfort all who are weighed down with grief, and write in their hearts your words of eternal life.
— Hear us . . .

Strengthen the weak in faith, and steady all who doubt.
— Hear us . . .

Extend your healing power to the sick, support the aged and comfort the dying with your saving presence.
— Hear us . . .

Collect for the week

The Lord be with you . . .

Free Prayer

General Collect

O God, source of light and of life, you have led us out of darkness into your marvellous light, from death into life and from slavery to freedom through the resurrection of your only Son. Lighten our hearts by the brightness of your Holy Spirit. Sanctify us entirely, body, mind and soul, in the communion of all the saints, through Christ our Lord,   — Amen.

Blessing

You sleeper, awake,
— Rise from the dead!
Upon you will shine the light,
— Jesus Christ, alleluia!

Let us bless the Lord, alleluia!
— We give our thanks to God, alleluia!

May the Lord of peace give us peace in all ways and at all times.
— Amen.

WEDNESDAY MORNING

Introduction

Give thanks to the Lord for he is good,
— For his love endures for ever, alleluia!

Open now the gates of justice:
— I will go in, I will give thanks.
This is the gate of the Lord,
— The just shall enter in.
I will give thanks, for you have heard me,
— You have saved me!

or:

Great and marvellous are your works, Master of all!
— Right and true are your ways, King of the nations.
Who would not give praise and glory to your Name?
— For you are holy, you alone!
All the nations will come and fall before you,
— For you have done wonders upon wonders.

Glory, worship, wisdom, thanksgiving! Alleluia!
— Adoration, power and strength to our God! Alleluia!

Psalm — Old Testament

Responses

O sing a new song to the Lord, for he has worked wonders.
+ His right hand has performed a great deed, raising us to
   holiness.
— O sing ...

The Lord has shown us salvation,
in the eyes of the nations revealed his justice.
— His right hand ...

All the ends of the earth have seen
the salvation of our God.
— His right hand . . .

Shout for the Lord, all the earth,
burst into shouts of joy!
— His right hand . . .

Let the rivers clap their hands,
and the mountains shout for joy!
— His right hand . . .

Glory to the Father, and the Son and the Holy Spirit.
— O sing a new song . . .

Gospel — Silence

Intercession

I know that my Redeemer is alive, alleluia!
— Alive for ever to intercede, alleluia!

God, Creator and Saviour, you have gathered the Church of
your Christ from the whole world, support her, that she may
everywhere bear witness faithfully.
— Hear us, victorious King.

Give peace to all the nations, and make them obedient to your
will, that all may enjoy the good things you bestow.
— Hear us, victorious King.

Be the salvation of our brothers and sisters who are oppressed,
and deliver all who are in prison for their faith.
— Hear us . . .

Comfort all who have lost heart, and lift up all who are lonely
and abandoned; give food to all who are hungry.
— Hear us . . .

Grant peace to the dying and reveal to them the light of your presence, and the power of your resurrection.
— Hear us . . .

Collect for the week
The Lord be with you . . .

Free Prayer

General Collect
Lord God, the well-spring of life, pour into our hearts the living water of your grace. By your light we see light. Increase our faith and grant that we may walk in the brightness of your presence, through Jesus Christ, your Son, our Lord, — Amen.

The Lord's Prayer
O Christ . . .

Blessing
Let us bless thee Lord, alleluia!
— We give our thanks to God, alleluia!

May the God of patience and of consolation grant us to live together after the pattern of our Lord Jesus Christ, so that with one heart and one voice we may give glory to God, the Father of our Lord Jesus Christ.
— Amen.

WEDNESDAY EVENING

Introduction

Give thanks to the Lord for he is good,
— For his love endures for ever, alleluia!

Close your ranks, branches in hand,
— And approach the altar.
You are my God, I give you thanks;
— My God, I give high praise!
I give you thanks, for you heard me,
— You were my salvation.

or:

The Lord has begun his reign in his Kingdom;
— Let us rejoice and be glad!
Glory to God, for now is the marriage of the Lamb;
— Happy the guests at the feast of the Lord.

Lord, give salvation, give victory!
— The Lord our God gives us light, alleluia!

Psalm — Epistle

Responses

The disciples were full of joy when they saw the Lord, alleluia, alleluia!
— The disciples . . .

Jesus said: Peace be among you.
— Alleluia, alleluia!

Glory to the Father, and the Son and the Holy Spirit.
— The disciples . . .

Silence — Hymn

Intercession

Stay with us, Lord, alleluia!
— For evening draws on, alleluia!

For all in the Church who work in the pursuit of truth, that they may rejoice in purity of heart, we pray:
— Hear us, Lord of glory!

For all the faithful in your Church, that they may fight the good fight and receive the good things promised in your Kingdom, we pray:
— Hear us...

For our country and our region, that you will save us from war and from all that destroys life, we pray:
— Hear us...

For the sick, that you will visit them and heal them, restoring and strengthening them for your glory, we pray:
— Hear us...

For the poor and the afflicted, for all who are tormented, distressed or persecuted, that you will help and comfort them, we pray:
— Hear us...

O God, our Father, you have given us in Christ a living hope, may your grace work in us all to the end, we pray:
— Hear us...

Collect for the week

The Lord be with you...

Free Prayer

General Collect

O Christ, you have seized the powers of death, and opened up the reign of life and immortality. We praise you, the light eternal, sun of the world to come. May our lives be hid with you in God, as heirs of your unending Kingdom,   — Amen.

Blessing

You sleeper, awake,
— Rise from the dead!
Upon you will shine the light,
— Jesus Christ, alleluia!

Let us bless the Lord, alleluia!
— We give our thanks to God, alleluia!

May our Lord Jesus Christ himself, and God our Father, who has loved us and given us by his grace eternal consolation and joyful hope, comfort our hearts and strengthen them in every good word and work.
— Amen.

THURSDAY MORNING

Introduction

Give thanks to the Lord for he is good,
— For his love endures for ever, alleluia!

In my distress I cried to the Lord,
— He heard me and set me free!
The Lord is on my side; no more fears!
— What can man do to me?
God is my help above all other;
— I have conquered the enemy!

or:

I saw the Holy City coming down from heaven:
— The dwelling-place of God with men.
They will be his People and God will be with them.
— He will wipe away every tear from their eyes.

Glory, worship, wisdom, thanksgiving! Alleluia!
— Adoration, power and strength to our God! Alleluia!

Psalm — Old Testament

Responses

The Lord watches over the faithful . . . (*as Monday Morning*)

Gospel — Silence

Intercession

I know that my Redeemer is alive, alleluia!
— Alive for ever to intercede, alleluia!

Lord, remember your Church, set firm on the foundation of
the apostles, spreading to the ends of the earth: bless all your
People:
— Hear us, Risen Lord!

Remember all who serve, that they may faithfully sow your Word among us, and be for your People examples of consecrated lives:
— Hear us ...

Provide for our needs, as is best for us; crown the year with your goodness for love of the poor and all the victims of starvation:
— Hear us ...

Visit us and heal us in your pity; restore and strengthen the sick, deliver them from their sufferings:
— Hear us ...

Come to the help of all who are suffering distress and oppression; free those unjustly imprisoned; give new heart to all who are weak and depressed:
— Hear us ...

Collect for the week
The Lord be with you ...

Free Prayer

General Collect
Lord God, look upon your Church and send us your Holy Spirit to unite us in one body, with one faith and one hope. So may we grow together into the perfect love of your Kingdom with Christ our Lord,   — Amen.

The Lord's Prayer
O Christ ...

Blessing
Let us bless the Lord, alleluia!
— We give our thanks to God, alleluia!

May the God of peace enable us to do his will in every kind of goodness, working in us what pleases him, through Jesus Christ, to whom be the glory for ever and ever.

— Amen.

THURSDAY EVENING

Introduction

As Monday evening, or:

Give thanks to the Lord for he is good,
— For his love endures for ever, alleluia!

See, I am making the whole world new.
— I am Alpha and Omega, the Beginning and the End.
To the thirsty I will give the water of life,
— The reward for the conqueror.

Lord, give salvation, give victory!
— The Lord our God gives us light, alleluia!

Psalm — Epistle

Responses

As on Monday evening

Silence — Hymn

Intercession

Stay with us, Lord, alleluia!
— For evening draws on, alleluia!

O Christ, we pray for your Church: sanctify us for the Coming
of your Kingdom.
— Son of the Living God, save us.

We pray you for all the ministers of your Church. As they
break the Bread of Life for your Family, may they too be
strengthened and fed.
— Son of the Living God . . .

We pray you for all your People, that they may live lives
worthy of their holy calling, and preserve the unity of the
Spirit in the bond of peace.
— Son . . .

We pray for all in power, that they may use their authority to become servants of justice, so that peace may reign among the nations of the world.
— Son . . .

We pray you for all who are enduring sickness, bereavement, oppressions, and exile, that you will give them comfort and help in their suffering.
— Son . . .

Collect for the week

The Lord be with you . . .

Free Prayer

General Collect

Creator of the universe, watch over us and keep us in the light of your presence. May our praise continually blend with that of all creation, until we come together to the eternal joys which you promise in your love, through Jesus Christ, our Lord,   — Amen.

Blessing

You sleeper, awake,
— Rise from the dead!
Upon you will shine the light,
— Jesus Christ, alleluia!

Let us bless the Lord, alleluia!
— We give our thanks to God, alleluia!

May the grace of our Lord Jesus Christ, the love of God and the communion of the Holy Spirit be with us all.
— Amen.

FRIDAY MORNING

Introduction

As Tuesday Morning, or:

Give thanks to the Lord for he is good,
— For his love endures for ever, alleluia!

I will give the conqueror fruit from the Tree of Life,
— Growing in the Garden of God.
He has nothing to fear from death.
— I will give him hidden manna.

Glory, worship, wisdom, thanksgiving! Alleluia!
— Adoration, power and strength to our God! Alleluia!

Psalm — Old Testament

Responses

As on Tuesday Morning

Gospel — Silence

Intercession

I know that my Redeemer is alive, alleluia!
— Alive for ever to intercede, alleluia!

Creator of the world, you have called us out of darkness into
light; you have opened our hearts to know you, the God of
all holiness:
— Hear us, Lord of Glory!

Be our help and our defender; save the oppressed, raise up the
fallen, show yourself to all in need, heal the sick:
— Hear us...

Teach those who have plenty to share your good gifts with their sisters and brothers in need and hunger; give freedom to prisoners, restore the weak, comfort the sorrowful:
— Hear us . . .

May all know that you are God alone, that Jesus Christ is your Son, and that we are your People in the Holy Spirit.
— Hear us . . .

Collect for the week
The Lord be with you . . .

Free Prayer

General Collect
Lord our God, the universe celebrates you and all creatures proclaim your power. Receive this morning the songs we raise and renew the gifts of your grace, through Jesus Christ, your Son, our Lord,   — Amen.

The Lord's Prayer
O Christ . . .

Blessing
Let us bless the Lord, alleluia!
— We give our thanks to God, alleluia!

May God the Father, and our Lord Jesus Christ, grant us Peace, and Love in believing.
— Amen.

FRIDAY EVENING

Introduction

As Tuesday Evening, or:

Give thanks to the Lord for he is good,
— For his love endures for ever, alleluia!

I will give the conqueror the Morning Star.
— He will be robed in white;
His name will never be removed from the Book of Life,
— I will answer for him in the presence of my Father.

Lord, give salvation, give victory!
— The Lord our God gives us light, alleluia!

Psalm — Epistle

Responses

As on Tuesday evening

Silence — Hymn

Intercession

Stay with us Lord, alleluia!
— For evening draws on, alleluia!

Lord, you have shown by your works that all will be made
perfect in love. You created the earth and you remain faithful
to every generation, just in your judgements, marvellous in
your strength:
— Save us, Lord of Glory!

Purify us in the light of your Truth, and guide our steps in
holiness of heart, that we may do what is right and pleasing
in your eyes.
— Save us . . .

Shine on us with your presence and peace; protect us with your strength, free us from sin and save us from all who hate us.
— Save us...

Give peace to us, and to all who live in the world; may the peoples of every nation worship and serve you in freedom and joy all the days of their life.
— Save us...

You have power to bring our prayers to pass, and you grant far more than we ask or desire, through our great High Priest, Jesus the Lord.
— Save us...

Collect for the week
The Lord be with you...

Free Prayer

General Collect
Lord Jesus Christ, you are the Shepherd and we are your flock; protect us all, and save us from every danger; fulfil your promise and be with us at every moment, that we may come to bless your Name in the light of our resurrection, in your Kingdom which will have no end,   — Amen.

Blessing
You sleeper, awake,
— Rise from the dead!
Upon you will shine the light,
— Jesus Christ, alleluia!

Let us bless the Lord, alleluia!
— We give our thanks to God, alleluia!

May the God of all grace, who has called us to his eternal glory in Christ, after we have suffered for a while, make us perfect, confirm and strengthen us; to him be the power for ever and ever.

— Amen.

SATURDAY MORNING

Introduction

As Wednesday Morning, or:

Give thanks to the Lord for he is good,
— For his love endures for ever, alleluia!

I will make the conqueror a Pillar,
— Standing in the House of the Lord;
I will write upon him the Name of the Lord,
— The Name of the City of God.

Glory, worship, wisdom, thanksgiving! Alleluia!
— Adoration, power and strength to our God! Alleluia!

Psalm — Old Testament

Responses

As on Wednesday Morning

Gospel — Silence

Intercession

I know that my Redeemer is alive, alleluia!
— Alive for ever to intercede, alleluia!

Help us, Lord, to root our lives firmly in the Faith: to find in
you our growth and fulfilment.
— Kyrie eleison.

Maintain our hearts and our minds in a common confession
of faith: make us one, that the world may believe your love.
— Kyrie eleison.

Be with the bishops and with all who serve your Church: may
they faithfully break for us the Bread of Life.
— Kyrie eleison.

Watch over all who believe, throughout the world: grant to each what is best, and the reward of your Kingdom.
— Kyrie eleison.

Give wisdom to the leaders of the nations: may they govern in the service of all.
— Kyrie eleison.

We remember all the apostles and the first witnesses to the Gospel: keep us in a communion of faith and of love with them.
— Kyrie eleison.

We remember all the prophets and the martyrs: direct our lives in the same spirit of service and of sacrifice.
— Kyrie eleison.

Collect for the week
The Lord be with you . . .

Free Prayer

General Collect
O God, you have wonderfully created us, and redeemed us still more wonderfully. Strengthen us by your Holy Spirit to resist sin and to receive your gifts of eternal life, through Jesus Christ, our Lord.
— Amen.

The Lord's Prayer
O Christ . . .

Blessing
Let us bless the Lord, alleluia!
— We give our thanks to God, alleluia!

May the peace of God, which surpasses all understanding, keep our hearts and our minds in Christ Jesus.
— Amen.

SATURDAY EVENING

Introduction

As Wednesday Evening, or:

Give thanks to the Lord for he is good,
— For his love endures for ever, alleluia!

I will give the conqueror a throne by my side,
— As I, when I conquered, with my Father;
This is the conqueror's reward;
— I will be his God, and he shall be my son.

Lord, give salvation, give victory!
— The Lord our God gives us light, alleluia!

Psalm — Epistle

Responses

As on Wednesday Evening

Silence — Hymn

Intercession

Stay with us Lord, alleluia!
— For evening draws on, alleluia!

O Christ, radiant Light, shining in our darkness. You are the most glorious of the children of men, the only Holy One among us sinners, the Source of Life who have sanctified our mortal nature:
— Son of the Living God, save us all!

You stooped low, and humbled yourself. You became obedient unto death. You walked the sorrowful road to the cross, and you call us to follow you in every moment of our lives, to death with you and to resurrection with you:
— Son . . .

You have saved us in our poverty, and won justification for us, to make us a holy nation, a People of kings and priests to God your Father:
— Son . . .

You grant us all the fulness of your grace through the gift of the Holy Spirit. Risen Lord, save us from death. Living Lord, make us sharers of your life. Conqueror, give us your victory!
— Son . . .

Burn in us all that is not kindled by your presence, and break in us all that would rebel against you, that our hearts may be fully your own as we wait for the day of your Revelation, when we shall be like you as we see you face to face.
— Son . . .

Collect for the week

The Lord be with you . . .

Free Prayer

General Collect

Lord God, keep your servants in health of soul and body. Deliver us from sorrow by the power of your resurrection, and be our joy now and every day of our lives,   — Amen.

Blessing

You sleeper, awake,
— Rise from the dead!
Upon you will shine the light,
— Jesus Christ, alleluia!

Let us bless the Lord, alleluia!
— We give our thanks to God, alleluia!

May almighty God bless us,
the Father, the Son and the Holy Spirit.
— Amen.

Introduction to the Gospel

Psalm or Hymn, followed by the next day's Gospel.

SUNDAY MORNING

Introduction

Alleluia! Christ is risen! Alleluia!
— He really is risen! Alleluia! Alleluia!

If we have died with Christ,
— With him also we shall live.
Risen from the dead, he will never die,
— Death has no power over him now.
His death was a death for sin,
— His life is a life for God.

Alleluia! Our hope is in him! Alleluia!
— He will take us into glory! Alleluia! Alleluia!

Psalm

Short Reading (Acts 10 40–43)

Song of Zechariah *(see Sunday Morning in Advent)*

Antiphon: I am the resurrection and the life, alleluia!

Collect for the week
The Lord be with you ...

SUNDAY EVENING

Introduction

Alleluia! Christ is risen! Alleluia!
— He really is risen! Alleluia! Alleluia!

The stone rejected by the builders,
— Is now the corner-stone.
This is the work of God,
— Marvellous in our eyes.
This is the day the Lord has made,
— Day of gladness, day of joy!

Alleluia! Our hope is in him! Alleluia!
— He will take us into glory! Alleluia! Alleluia!

Psalm — Epistle

Song of Mary *(see Sunday Evening in Advent)*

Antiphon: He is risen! You shall see him, as he said!
Alleluia!

Silence — Hymn

Praise

O Christ our Saviour, begotten of the Father before time
began. You put on the flesh of our humanity. You were
crucified and buried; and now you have risen from the dead
as you promised. We worship you, Almighty Lord!
— Glory, victorious Christ!

Now, as daylight is fading, we offer you our worship: to you,
the eternal light! When the hour had come, you shone out in
our mortal flesh as in a mirror, to enlighten the world and to
reveal to all the light of the resurrection:
— Glory . . .

We rejoice in your Cross, we celebrate your resurrection. By your death you destroyed death, and you have restored us to life by your gift of immortality:
— Glory ...

Lord, you will return to judge the world: have mercy on us sinners. In you we take refuge, before you we bow down. To you we pray, for you are our God and our Saviour:
— Glory ...

Collect for the week
The Lord be with you ...

Free Prayer

General Collect
Lord, by your cross you have broken death; you turned to joy the grief of your friends, you opened Paradise to a robber and you charged your apostles to proclaim the resurrection to all mankind. Have mercy, Lord, on us all, now and in the day of your Appearing, for you reign for ever and ever,
— Amen.

Blessing
You sleeper, awake,
— Rise from the dead!
Upon you will shine the light,
— Jesus Christ, alleluia!

Let us bless the Lord, alleluia!
— We give our thanks to God, alleluia!

May the Lord bless us, the Maker of heaven and earth.
— Amen.

ASCENSION

Introduction

Jesus Christ is Lord!
— To the glory of God the Father!

Jesus, by nature divine,
would not retain for himself
his rank as equal with God.

He poured out his glory in love,
becoming a humble slave,
and living the life of a man.

And human in every way,
he abased himself still more, obedient to death,
death on a cross.

So God has exalted him high,
and given to him the Name,
the greatest of all the names,

So that at Jesus' Name
every knee should bend low
in heaven, on earth, in the depths.

And every tongue proclaim:
Jesus Christ is Lord,
to the glory of God the Father!

Psalm (23, 46 or 96) — Old Testament or Epistle

Responses

O God, arise above the heavens,
+ On the earth, your glory!
— O God . . .

Have mercy, O God, mercy on me,
my soul finds shelter in you.
— On the earth . . .

I shelter in the shadow of your wings,
till the storm has passed.
— On the earth . . .

I call on God the Most High,
to send from heaven and save me.
— On the earth . . .

Your love is high as the heavens,
your faithfulness, as the clouds.
— On the earth . . .

Glory to the Father, and the Son and the Holy Spirit.
— O God, arise . . .

Gospel (Morning) — Silence — Hymn

Intercession

Arise, O Lord, in your strength,
— We will sing and play for your glory!

Let us pray with joy to Christ at the right hand of the Father,
saying:
— You are the King of Glory!

You have raised the weakness of our flesh, heal us from our
sins: restore us to the full dignity of our life.
— You are the King of Glory!

May our faith lead us to the Father: as we follow the road
you trod.
— You . . .

You have promised to draw all to yourself: let no one of us stay separate from your Body.
— You . . .

Grant that by our longing we may join you in your Kingdom: where your humanity and ours is glorified.
— You . . .

You are true God, and you will be our judge: so lead us to contemplate your tender mercy.
— You . . .

Collect for the Day
The Lord be with you . . .

Free Prayer

General Collect
Almighty God, we exult in thankful joy; your Son is really risen and has entered the glory of your love. By his victory, we too are sure of victory; may this be our hope and our goal, all the days of our life, through Jesus Christ who lives and reigns now and for ever,   — Amen.

The Lord's Prayer (Morning)
O Christ . . .

Blessing
Risen with Christ, let us seek the realities of the Spirit:
— Our life is hidden with Christ in God.
When Christ, our Life, appears,
— We shall appear with him in glory! Alleluia! Alleluia!

Let us bless the Lord, alleluia!
— We give our thanks to God, alleluia!

May grace be with all who love our Lord Jesus Christ in life incorruptible.
— Amen.

PENTECOST: MORNINGS

(From Pentecost until the following Sunday)

Introduction

Send forth your Spirit, Lord,
— Renew the face of the earth.
Creator Spirit, come,
— Inflame our waiting hearts.
Your Spirit fills the world,
— And knows our every word.

Glory to God our Father,
— To Jesus Christ, the Son,
To you, O Holy Spirit,
— Now and for evermore.
You are, you were, you come,
— Eternal, living God!

Psalm — Old Testament

Responses

Come Holy Spirit,
From heaven shine forth with your glorious light!
— Come . . .

Come, Father of the poor; come generous Spirit;
Come, light of our hearts!
— From heaven . . .

Perfect Comforter! Wonderful Refreshment!
You make peace to dwell in our soul.
In our labour, you offer rest;
in temptation, strength;
and in our sadness, consolation.
— From heaven . . .

Most kindly, warming Light! Enter the inmost depth of our hearts, for we are faithful to you.
Without your presence, we have nothing worthy, nothing pure.
— From heaven . . .

Wash away our sin, send rain upon our dry ground,
heal our wounded souls.
With warmth bend our rigidity, inflame our apathy,
and direct our wandering feet.
— From heaven . . .

On all who put their trust in you, and receive you in faith,
shower all your gifts.
Grant that they may grow in you, and persevere to the end;
give them lasting joy! Alleluia!
— Come, Holy Spirit, From heaven . . .

Gospel — Silence

Praise

The Spirit joins with our spirit, alleluia!
— He declares that we are children of God, alleluia!

Holy Spirit, Creator! In the beginning, you moved over the waters, and from your breath all creatures drew their life. Without you, every living creature turns to dust:
— Holy Spirit, come!

Holy Spirit, Counsellor! By your inspiration the People of God and the prophets spoke and acted in faith. You clothed them in your power, to be bearers of your Word.
— Holy Spirit, come!

Holy Spirit, Power! You overshadowed the Virgin Mary, to make her the mother of the Son of God. You prepared a pure dwelling to receive him.
— Holy Spirit, come!

215

Holy Spirit, Sanctifier! By you, Jesus grew in wisdom and grace. On the day of his baptism, you descended on him as a dove to consecrate him and you armed him with power to bear witness to the Father.
— Holy Spirit, come!

Collect for the week

The Lord be with you . . .

Free Prayer

General Collect

Father, of your infinite goodness, set us aflame with that fire of the Spirit Christ brought upon the earth and longed to see ablaze, for he lives and reigns with you and the Spirit now and for ever,   — Amen.

The Lord's Prayer

O Christ . . .

Blessing

Let us bless the Lord, alleluia!
— We give our thanks to God, alleluia!

May the grace of our Lord Jesus Christ, the love of God the Father and the communion of the Holy Spirit, be with us all.
— Amen.

PENTECOST: EVENINGS

Introduction: as Mornings

Psalm — Epistle

Responses

You fill the whole world, O Spirit of Power! Alleluia! Alleluia!
— You fill...

You know every word, since all life lives in you.
— Alleluia! Alleluia!

Glory to the Father, and the Son and the Holy Spirit.
— You fill...

Silence — Hymn

Intercession

The Spirit comes to assist our weakness, alleluia!
— He himself intercedes for us, alleluia!

Living God! Come and make our bodies the temples of your
Holy Spirit. Baptise with fire your whole Church, that we may
stand in the world as a pillar of your love.
— Strengthen us, Holy Spirit!

Give to us all the fruits of the Spirit: love for all, joy, peace,
patience, kindness, faithfulness.
— Strengthen...

May your Spirit speak through your servants who live by your
Word of truth.
— Strengthen...

Send the Comforter to all who are passing through adversity,
or are the victims of human wickedness.
— Strengthen...

Preserve from hatred and war every nation, every people, and create a new brotherhood among us by the power of your communion.
— Strengthen ...

Holy Spirit, Lord and Source of Life, giver of many gifts:
— Strengthen ...

Spirit of wisdom and of knowledge; Spirit of counsel and of might:
— Strengthen ...

Spirit of understanding and of prayer; Spirit of obedience:
— Strengthen ...

Collect for the week

The Lord be with you ...

Free Prayer

General Collect: as Mornings

Blessing

Come, Holy Spirit,
— Inflame our waiting hearts!
Burn us with your love,
— Renew us in your life.
Let us bless the Lord, alleluia!
— We give our thanks to God, alleluia!

May Almighty God bless us,
the Father, the Son and the Holy Spirit.
— Amen.

On Saturday: Introduction to the Gospel

Psalm or Hymn

Reading of the Gospel for Trinity Sunday ...

Song of the Spirit

The Father will give you another Comforter,
— The Spirit of Truth, to be always with you.
The Holy Spirit will teach you everything,
— He will recall to you all I said, alleluia!

When the Spirit of Truth comes,
— He will lead you into all the truth;
For he will not speak by himself,
— But all that he hears, he will tell, alleluia!

Ordinary Days

after Epiphany

after Pentecost

This liturgy is celebrated from the Monday after the Sunday of the Baptism of Christ (Epiphany 1) until the Tuesday before Lent (Eve of Ash Wednesday, Shrove Tuesday); then, from the Monday after Trinity Sunday (Pentecost 1) until the Saturday before Advent. Week 1 and Week 2 alternate.

MONDAY MORNING I

Introduction

Lord, open my lips,
— And my mouth shall proclaim your praise.
O God, come and help me,
— Lord, support and save me.

To you, Lord, I call:
— My rock, be not deaf;
If you kept silence,
— I should be as dead.

Hear the voice of my prayer
— When I cry for help,
Lord, when I lift my hands,
— Pleading in your presence.

Psalm — Old Testament

Responses

To you, Lord, I pray, you hear me every morning;
+ In the morning I rise for you, I long to see you come.
— To you, Lord . . .

O Lord, hear my words,
consider my pleading.
Hear my cry for help,
my King and my God:
— In the morning I rise for you, I long to see you come.

By the grace of your great love
I enter your house;
Low before your sanctuary
I bow, and adore:
— In the morning . . .

Great joy for all you shelter,
songs of praise for ever;
you shield and protect from harm
all who love your name:
— In the morning . . .

Lord, you bless the good,
your love defends them from evil:
— In the morning . . .

Glory to the Father, and the Son and the Holy Spirit.
— To you, Lord, I pray . . .

Gospel — Silence

Intercession

Satisfy us with your love in the morning:
— And we will live this day in joy and praise.

————

Be our help and our salvation, have pity on us and keep us,
Lord, by your grace:
— Kyrie eleison (*or:* Lord, have mercy).

Let us ask the Lord for a day of fulfilment and of peace:
— Kyrie eleison.

Let us ask the Lord for what is good and profitable for our
lives, and for peace in the world:
— Kyrie eleison.

Let us ask the Lord for grace to spend our whole lives in
peace and faithfulness:
— Kyrie eleison.

Let us ask the Lord for a peaceful end to our lives, without
pain or reproach, and for his mercy at the last judgement:
— Kyrie eleison.

In the communion of the saints let us offer one another and our whole lives to Christ our God:
— Kyrie eleison.

Collect for the week

The Lord be with you, — And also with you.
Let us pray to the Lord: *(silence, then the collect)* — Amen.

Free Prayer

General Collect

God most holy, we give you thanks for bringing us out of the shadow of night into the light of morning; and we ask you for the joy of spending this day in your service, so that when evening comes, we may once more give you thanks, through Jesus Christ, your Son, our Lord,   — Amen.

The Lord's Prayer

O Christ, remember us in your Kingdom:
— Lord, teach us to pray: Our Father . . .

Blessing

Let us bless the Lord,
— We give our thanks to God.

May the God of hope fill us with all joy and all peace in believing, that we may be overflowing with hope through the power of the Holy Spirit.
— Amen.

MONDAY EVENING I

Introduction

Lord, open my lips,
— And my mouth shall proclaim your praise.
O God, come and help me,
— Lord, support and save me.

The Lord is my strength and my shield,
— On him my heart relies;
I have been helped, my health is renewed;
— I give thanks with all my heart.

The Lord is the strength of his People,
— A stronghold of salvation for his Christ.
Save your People, bless your heritage,
— Carry them and guide them for ever!

Psalm — Epistle

Responses

O Christ, Son of the Living God, have pity on us.
— O Christ . . .

Lord, enthroned at the right hand of God,
— Have pity on us.

Glory to the Father, and the Son and the Holy Spirit.
— O Christ, Son of the Living God, have pity on us.

Silence — Hymn

Intercession

Let my prayer rise before you like incense;
— And my hands like an evening offering.

———

For your peace, and for the ransom of our lives in your love:
— Lord, we pray.

For our community, and for the unity of the Church in all the world:
— Lord we pray.

For those who govern us, that they may receive your aid to triumph over all injustice and evil:
— Lord, we pray.

For our country, our district, our town (city *or* village); for the Christians living here. May they serve their neighbours in friendship and hope:
— Lord, we pray.

For all whose lives bear witness to Christ; for those who minister in the Church; for those who live with the poor, the defenceless, with foreigners and the oppressed; for those who have asked us to remember them in our prayers:
— Lord, wc pray.

For the old and the frail; for the sick, the sad; may all receive from you new health and salvation:
— Lord, we pray.

Collect for the week

The Lord be with you, — And also with you.
Let us pray to the Lord: *(silence, then the collect)* — Amen.

Free Prayer

General Collect

Stay with us, Father of light, and protect us through the silent hours of this night; we are wearied by the changes of this passing world: may we rest in your eternal changelessness, for you are faithful and your love never varies, through Jesus Christ, your Son, our Lord,   — Amen.

Blessing

Let us bless the Lord,
— We give our thanks to God.

May the God of peace sanctify us wholly, keeping us blame-less in body, mind and soul for the Coming of our Lord Jesus Christ.
— Amen.

TUESDAY MORNING I

Introduction

Lord, open my lips,
— And my mouth shall proclaim your praise.
O God, come and help me,
— Lord, support and save me.

My soul pines and sighs
— For the courts of the Lord;
My heart and my flesh shout for joy
— To you, O Living God!

The sparrow has found a home
— And the swallow a nest for her young:
Your altars, Lord of all the worlds,
— My King and my God!

Happy are they who live in your house,
— They praise you for ever and ever;
Happy men whose strength is in you,
— Hearts strong for the climb to your city.

Passing through the Valley of the Weeper,
— They make it a place of wells;
They will go from height to height,
— God will appear to them in Zion.

Psalm — Old Testament

Responses

In the evening tears,
 + In the morning shouts of joy!
— In the evening . . .

Glory to you, for you have helped me up,
my enemies gloat no longer.
— In the morning shouts of joy!

227

Make music for the Lord, all who love him,
praise the memory of his holiness:
— In the morning . . .

You have turned my mourning to dancing,
taken my sackcloth and clothed me with joy:
— In the morning . . .

My heart will continually praise you,
Lord my God, I will laud you for ever:
— In the morning . . .

Glory to the Father, and the Son and the Holy Spirit.
— In the evening tears, in the morning shouts of joy!

Gospel — Silence

Intercession

Satisfy us with your love in the morning,
— And we will live this day in joy and praise.

————

We pray for all who believe and who have confessed Jesus
Christ as Lord; — Strengthen us in the knowledge of your
truth:
— Kyrie eleison.

We pray to you for all the nations; — May they know you as
Creator and Father, and Jesus Christ your only Son:
— Kyrie eleison.

We pray to you for all in authority; — May we be governed
in peace for the good of the universal Church and of all
mankind:
— Kyrie eleison.

We pray to you for all who enjoy freedom, and for those who
are oppressed; — Show your kindness and extend your goodness to all, and lead their steps to yourself:
— Kyrie eleison.

We pray to you for all who are suffering, for prisoners and the victims of society; — Comfort them, Source of all comfort:
— Kyrie eleison.

We pray to you for the sick; — Give them health of body and soul:
— Kyrie eleison.

Collect for the week

The Lord be with you, — And also with you.
Let us pray to the Lord: *(silence, then the collect)* — Amen.

Free Prayer

General Collect

Almighty God, you have given us grace to offer our common intercessions, and you have promised that when two or three meet in your name, you will grant their requests. Fulfil, Lord, the desires and prayers of your servants, as you judge best for us: grant us in this world knowledge of your truth, and in the world to come life eternal, through Jesus Christ, your Son our Saviour,   — Amen.

The Lord's Prayer

O Christ, remember us in your Kingdom,
— Lord, teach us to pray: Our Father ...

Blessing

Let us bless the Lord,
— We give our thanks to God.

May the Lord bless us and keep us; may Christ smile upon us and give us his grace; may he unveil his face to us and bring us his peace.
— Amen.

TUESDAY EVENING I

Introduction

Lord, open my lips,
— And my mouth shall proclaim your praise.
O God, come and help me,
— Lord, support and save me.

God be gracious to us and bless us
— And smile down upon us;
The world will acknowledge your ways,
— All nations your power to save.

Let the peoples rejoice and sing,
— For you judge the world justly;
You judge the nations with equity,
— You govern the nations on the earth.

The earth has yielded her harvest,
— God, our God has blessed us.
Lord, bless us! May you be worshipped
— To all the ends of the earth.

Psalm — Epistle

Responses

Incline my heart to your commandments,
revive me by your Word.
— Incline . . .

Fulfil your promise to your servant.
— Revive me by your Word.

Glory to the Father, and the Son and the Holy Spirit.
— Incline my heart . . .

Silence — Hymn

Intercession

Let my prayer rise before you like incense,
— And my hands like an evening offering.

———

Let us implore the mercy of the Lord:
— Deliver us, O Lord.

God of tenderness and compassion:
— Deliver us, O Lord.

From injustice, from hatred and every spirit of impurity:
— Deliver us, O Lord.

From war and famine, from disease and disaster:
— Deliver us, O Lord.

By the mystery of your incarnation, by your coming into the world:
— Deliver us, O Lord.

By your birth in poverty, by your baptism and your fasting in the desert:
— Deliver us, O Lord.

By your Cross and your Passion, by your death and your burial:
— Deliver us, O Lord.

By your resurrection from the dead, by your ascension into glory:
— Deliver us, O Lord.

By the coming of the Holy Spirit the Comforter, and on the Day of judgement:
— Deliver us, O Lord.

We are sinners, give us pardon and true repentance of heart:
— Deliver us, O Lord.

Collect for the week

The Lord be with you, — And also with you.
Let us pray to the Lord: *(silence, then the cc'lect)* — Amen.

Free Prayer

General Collect

O God, your light never fades; dawn in our hearts and strengthen us in the inner man by the brightness of your presence; may darkness find no entry in us, through Jesus Christ, our Lord,   — Amen.

Blessing

Let us bless the Lord,
— We give our thanks to God.

May the Lord of peace give us peace in all ways and at all times.
— Amen.

WEDNESDAY MORNING I

Introduction

Lord, open my lips,
— And my mouth shall proclaim your praise.
O God, come and help me,
— Lord, support and save me.

The Lord reigns, clothed in majesty,
The Lord is robed in power,
— He has girt up his loins with power.

You built the world immovable;
Your throne stands firm from the beginning,
— For all time you are the Lord.

Lord, the rivers are out in flood,
The rivers roll their thunder,
— The rivers shout their noise.

Greater than the roar of the ocean,
Transcending the surge of the sea,
— The Lord reigns on high.

Your commands are ever right;
Holiness is the beauty of your house,
— Lord, for ever and ever.

Psalm — Old Testament

Responses

My time is in your hand, deliver me;
+ Smile on your servant with the light of your love.
— My time . . .

In you, Lord, I take shelter,
bend over me quickly and hear me.
— Smile on your servant with the light of your love.

You are my rock and my rampart,
guide me and lead, for your name's sake.
— Smile on your servant . . .

I do rely on the Lord;
I sing and exult in your love!
— Smile on your servant . . .

Take heart, take courage once more,
all who hope in the Lord!
— Smile on your servant . . .

Glory to the Father, and the Son and the Holy Spirit.
— My time is in your hand . . .

Gospel — Silence

Intercession

Satisfy us with your love in the morning,
— And we will live this day in joy and praise.

———

Lord, have mercy on us:
— Heal our souls, for we have sinned against you.

Return, O Lord! How long?
— Have pity on your servants.

Your love, Lord, rest upon us:
— As our hope is in you.

Let us pray for all who are called to lead the Church:
— God keep them, and give them happiness in their service.

Lord, come and guide the nations:
— Hear us when we call to you.

Save your People, bless your heritage:
— Guide them and carry them for ever.

Collect for the week

The Lord be with you, — And also with you.
Let us pray to the Lord: *(silence, then the collect)* — Amen.

Free Prayer

General Collect

Eternal Word of the Father; for our salvation you became one with us in everything but sin. Give us the light of your liberating word, may we not only hear it, but act upon it; and so lead us into God's Kingdom where you live and reign for ever,
— Amen.

The Lord's Prayer

O Christ, remember us in your Kingdom,
— Lord, teach us to pray: Our Father . . .

Blessing

Let us bless the Lord,
— We give our thanks to God.

May the God of patience and of consolation grant us to live together after the pattern of our Lord Jesus Christ, so that with one heart and one voice we may give glory to God, the Father of our Lord Jesus Christ.
— Amen.

WEDNESDAY EVENING I

Introduction

Lord, open my lips,
— And my mouth shall proclaim your praise.
O God, come and help me,
— Lord, support and save me.

I lift my eyes to the hills:
where shall I find help?
— Help comes from the Lord,
    maker of heaven and earth.

He will not leave you to stumble,
your guardian never sleeps.
— No. The guardian of Israel
    never falls asleep.

The Lord guards you and shades you;
with him close at hand,
— The sun will not strike you by day,
    nor the moon at night-time.

The Lord will guard you from harm,
he will guard your soul.
— He guards your goings and comings,
    now and evermore.

Psalm — Epistle

Responses

For ever, Lord, your Word: unshaken in the heavens.
— For ever, Lord . . .

Your truth stands from age to age.
— Unshaken in the heavens.

Glory to the Father, and the Son and the Holy Spirit.
— For ever, Lord, your Word: unshaken in the heavens.

Silence — Hymn

Intercession

Let my prayer rise before you like incense:
— And my hands like an evening offering.

————

Let us pray in faith to God our Father, to his Son Jesus Christ
and the Holy Spirit:
— O Lord, hear and have mercy (*or:* Kyrie eleison).

For the Church of the living God throughout the whole world,
let us ask the riches of his grace:
— O Lord, hear and have mercy.

For all who faithfully communicate the Word of truth, let us
ask the infinite wisdom of Christ:
— O Lord, hear and have mercy.

For all who consecrate themselves, body and soul, to the
Kingdom of God; for all who are struggling along the way of
Christ, let us implore the gifts of the Spirit:
— O Lord, hear and have mercy.

For all who govern the nations, that they may bring about a
reign of justice and of peace, let us ask the strength of God:
— O Lord, hear and have mercy.

For scholars and research-workers, that their studies may
serve the well-being of all mankind, let us ask the light of the
Lord:
— O Lord, hear and have mercy.

For all who work in harsh and inhuman conditions, that their dignity may be recognized and respected, and that they may receive a right reward for the work they do, let us ask help of God:

— O Lord, hear and have mercy.

Collect for the week

The Lord be with you, — And also with you.
Let us pray to the Lord: *(silence, then the collect)* — Amen.

Free Prayer

General Collect

O God, your name is blessed from the rising of the sun to its setting; fill our hearts with knowledge of yourself and our mouths with your praise, that from East to West all may sing your glory, with one voice and with one accord, in Jesus Christ, your Son, our Lord,   — Amen.

Blessing

Let us bless the Lord,
— We give our thanks to God.

May our Lord Jesus Christ himself, and God our Father who has loved us, and given us by his grace eternal consolation and joyful hope, comfort our hearts and strengthen them in every good word and work.
— Amen.

THURSDAY MORNING I

Introduction

Lord, open my lips,
— And my mouth shall proclaim your praise.
O God, come and help me,
— Lord, support and save me.

Sing to the Lord, a new song,
Sing to the Lord, all the earth,
— Sing to the Lord, bless his name!

Proclaim his salvation day by day,
Tell his glory to the nations,
— His wonders to all peoples!

God is great and worthy of all praise,
To be feared above all gods:
— The gods of the nations are nothing.

It is God who made the heavens,
Glory and majesty attend him,
— Strength and beauty in his sanctuary.

Render to the Lord, children of all nations,
Render to the Lord glory and power,
— Render to the Lord the glory of his name.

Psalm — Old Testament

Responses

The eyes of the Lord are on the just,
+ To the broken-hearted the Lord is near.
— The eyes of the Lord . . .

I will bless the Lord at all times,
his praise always on my lips.
— To the broken-hearted the Lord is near.

Look to him and you will shine,
no shame clouding your face.
— To the broken-hearted . . .

Who is longing for life,
and for many days of joy?
— To the broken-hearted . . .

The Lord comes to ransom his servants,
he protects them body and soul.
— To the broken-hearted . . .

Glory to the Father, and the Son and the Holy Spirit.
— The eyes of the Lord . . .

Gospel — Silence

Intercession

Satisfy us with your love in the morning,
— And we will live this day in joy and praise.

———

Let us pray for the peace of the world: The Lord grant
that we may live together in justice and faith.
— Lord, hear our prayer.

Let us pray for the holy Church throughout the world: The
Lord keep her unshaken, founded upon the rock of his Word
until the end of time.
— Lord, hear our prayer.

Let us pray for children and young people: The Lord
strengthen them in their vocation.
— Lord, hear our prayer.

Let us pray for the sick: The Lord deliver them and restore
the strength they need.
— Lord, hear our prayer.

Let us pray for all who are condemned to exile, prison, harsh treatment, or hard labour for the name of Christ: The Lord support them and keep them true in faith.
— Lord, hear our prayer.

Remembering all the witnesses and martyrs of the faith, all who have given their lives for God, and in communion with our brothers and sisters who have fallen asleep in Christ: Let us commit ourselves and one another to the living God through Christ our Lord.
— Lord, hear our prayer.

Collect for the week

The Lord be with you, — And also with you.
Let us pray to the Lord: *(silence, then the collect)* — Amen.

Free Prayer

General Collect

O Christ, in the brightness of your face we behold the glory of the Father. By your grace direct our steps in your way, in communion with your whole People, for you are Lord for ever, — Amen.

The Lord's Prayer

O Christ, remember us in your Kingdom,
— Lord, teach us to pray: Our Father . . .

Blessing

Let us bless the Lord,
— We give our thanks to God.

May the God of peace enable us to do his will in every kind of goodness, working in us what pleases him, through Jesus Christ to whom be the glory for ever and ever.
— Amen.

THURSDAY EVENING I

Introduction

Lord, open my lips,
— And my mouth shall proclaim your praise.
O God, come and help me,
— Lord, support and save me.

To you, God in heaven,
— I look, and wait,
My eyes like a slave's, intent
— on the hand of his master.

Or like the eyes of a maid
— on the hand of her mistress,
Our gaze is fixed on the Lord,
— waiting for his kindness.

Show kindness, O Lord, show kindness,
— We have suffered contempt enough;
Too long now have we suffered
— from the disdain of the proud.

Psalm — Epistle

Responses

I call from my heart, answer me, my God.
— I call . . .

I will keep your commandments.
— Answer me, my God.

Glory to the Father, and the Son and the Holy Spirit.
— I call from my heart, answer me, my God.

Silence — Hymn

Intercession

Let my prayer rise before you like incense,
— And my hands like an evening offering.

———

Filled with your kindness and your peace, with all our hearts
and all our minds we pray to you:
— Kyrie eleison (*or:* O Lord, hear and have mercy).

For the unity of the Church, for those who cannot believe, and
for peace among the nations, we pray to you:
— Kyrie eleison.

For us who are weak in faith, help our unbelief, and for all
who look for your presence, we pray to you:
— Kyrie eleison.

For this country and the life of all living here, we pray to you:
— Kyrie eleison.

That all may be sure of finding proper work, and of being able
to live by it, we pray to you:
— Kyrie eleison.

For all who are in prison, condemned or exiled, we pray to
you:
— Kyrie eleison.

For all the sick, in body or mind, we pray to you:
— Kyrie eleison.

That in your Church we may become signs of brotherly love
and of new hope, we pray to you:
— Kyrie eleison.

Collect for the week

The Lord be with you, — And also with you.
Let us pray to the Lord: *(silence, then the collect)* — **Amen.**

Free Prayer

General Collect

O Lord, you promise that all whose hearts are clear shall see God; dispel the darkness and confusion of our hearts, and in your light we shall see eternal light, now and ever, — Amen.

Blessing

Let us bless the Lord,
— We give our thanks to God.

May the grace of our Lord Jesus Christ, the love of God and the communion of the Holy Spirit be with us all.
— Amen.

FRIDAY MORNING I

Introduction

Blessed be our God at all times,
now and always and for ever and ever:
— Amen.

Come, let us fall down and worship God our King:
— Come, let us fall down and worship Christ, our King and
   our God.

Come, let us fall down and worship Christ among us, our King
and our God.
— God, holy; God, strong and holy; God, holy and immortal:
   have pity on us.

Psalm — Old Testament

Responses

In my mouth he has put a new song:
+ Praise to our God!
— In my mouth . . .

I hoped in the Lord with a great hope,
he stooped down, and he heard me cry:
— Praise to our God!

Many shall see and shall fear him,
they shall believe in the Lord:
— Praise to our God!

My God, I have loved your law
from the depths of my heart:
— Praise to our God!

I have proclaimed the justice of the Lord
in the great assembly:
— Praise to our God!

Glory to the Father, and the Son and the Holy Spirit.
— In my mouth . . .

Gospel — Silence

Intercession

Christ loves us and has washed us from our sins by his blood:
— He has made us a People of priests for God our Father.

———

Let us pray for the whole Church, for the faithful and all who serve, that the Lord give us the grace of lives wholly consecrated to his will:
— O Lord, answer our prayer.

Let us pray for all who hate us or persecute us for Christ's sake; may the Lord calm their hatred against us, filling their hearts and ours with his generous love:
— O Lord, answer our prayer.

Let us pray for all who are lonely, weary, overworked or depressed, for all who are destitute and have no-one to turn to; may the Lord protect and save in his love all who can only hope in him:
— O Lord, answer our prayer.

Let us pray for one another, and for all who are absent from us now; the Lord keep us in his grace to the end, preserve us from falling, and gather us together in his Kingdom:
— O Lord, answer our prayer.

Remembering all the witnesses and martyrs of the faith, and all who have given their lives for God, and in communion with all our brothers and sisters who have fallen asleep in Christ, let us commit ourselves and one another to the living God through his Christ:
— O Lord, answer our prayer.

Collect for the week

The Lord be with you, — And also with you.
Let us pray to the Lord; *(silence, then the collect)* — Amen.

Free Prayer

General Collect

Lord Jesus, on the morning of your death you offered yourself
to the mocking of your enemies; visit us, we pray you, with
your love; may we find peace in the difficulties of our lives and
joy in whatever serves to praise you, our Lord for ever and
ever,   — Amen.

The Lord's Prayer

O Christ, remember us in your Kingdom,
— Lord, teach us to pray: Our Father . . .

Blessing

Let us bless the Lord,
— We give our thanks to God.

May God the Father, and our Lord Jesus Christ, grant us
peace and love in believing.
— Amen.

FRIDAY EVENING I

Introduction

Blessed be our God at all times,
now and always and for ever and ever:
— Amen.

Come, let us fall down and worship God our King:
— Come, let us fall down and worship Christ, our King and
our God.

Come, let us fall down and worship Christ among us, our
King and our God.
— God, holy; God, strong and holy; God, holy and immortal:
have pity on us.

Psalm — Epistle

Responses

Heal my soul, for I have sinned against you.
— Heal my soul . . .

I said: Have pity on me, Lord.
— For I have sinned against you.

Glory to the Father, and the Son and the Holy Spirit.
— Heal my soul, for I have sinned against you.

Silence — Hymn

Intercession

Christ loves us and has washed us from our sins by his blood:
— He has made us a People of priests for God our Father.

———

For the universal Church, that the Lord give her everywhere
peace and unity, perseverance in her faith and her mission,
let us pray to the Lord:
— O Lord, hear our prayer.

For the whole People of God, that each one may be a servant of Christ truly and faithfully, let us pray to the Lord:
— O Lord, hear our prayer.

For those who are drawing near to the light of faith, that the Lord guide their steps into the communion of the Body of Christ, let us pray to the Lord:
— O Lord, hear our prayer.

For all mankind, and for each individual person, for those who are lonely, sick, hungry, persecuted, ignored, let us pray to the Lord:
— O Lord, hear our prayer.

Collect for the week

The Lord be with you, — And also with you.
Let us pray to the Lord; *(silence, then the collect)* — Amen.

Free Prayer

General Collect

Almighty God, your glory was manifested in the Cross of our Lord Jesus Christ; may the contemplation of this love fill us with joy and hope, for he lives and reigns now and for ever,
— Amen.

Blessing

Let us bless the Lord,
— We give our thanks to God.

May the God of all grace, who has called us to his eternal glory in Christ; after we have suffered for a while, make us perfect, confirm and strengthen us; to him be the power for ever and ever.
— Amen.

Introduction

Lord, open my lips,
— And my mouth shall proclaim your praise.
O God, come and help me,
— Lord, support and save me.

Sing to the Lord, all the earth,
Serve the Lord with gladness,
— Come before him with songs of joy.

Know that he, the Lord, is God;
He made us, and we are his,
— His People and the sheep of his flock.

Come to his gates and give thanks,
Enter his courts, praising him,
— Give thanks to him and bless his name.

How good, how good is the Lord!
His love lasts for ever.
— He is faithful from age to age.

Psalm — Old Testament

Song of Zechariah

Antiphon:

Through the love in the heart of our God,
the Rising Sun has come to us.

Blessed be the Lord God of Israel,
coming to ransom his People;

Raising up saving power
in the house of his servant David,
as he said by the mouth of his prophets,
his saints in the times of old:

He sets us free from oppression,
free from the hands of our foes;
his bond of love with our fathers,
his covenant binding for ever;

His oath to our father Abraham,
assuring us, that liberated from fear,
delivered from all oppression,
we serve him in goodness and love,
before him, throughout our days.

And you, to be called his prophet,
will walk in the presence of God,
to prepare the ways he shall come,
announcing his People's salvation
with pardon for all their sins.

Through the love in the heart of our God,
the rising Sun will come to us,
shining on those in the dark
who lie in the shadow of death,
and guiding our steps into peace.

Gospel — Silence

Intercession

Satisfy us with your love in the morning,
— And we will live this day in joy and praise.

————

By Christ our Lord, your beloved Son; by his birth and his
life, by his words and his miracles, by his sufferings, by his
death on the Cross and by his resurrection from among the
dead, Lord, make us strong:
— Kyrie eleison (*or:* Lord, have mercy).

In prosperity and in calamity, in temptations, in trials, at our
last hour and on the day of judgement, Lord, make us strong:
— Kyrie eleison.

We pray you to bless and guide your Church throughout the world; may we grow in unity, in faith and in love:
— Kyrie eleison.

Lead us in the ways of your justice, that all may have their proper share in the good things you give us, and may our lives be filled with your marvellous presence:
— Kyrie eleison.

Raise the fallen and strengthen those who stand; grant to all the weak and those in trouble your consolation and your help:
— Kyrie eleison.

Collect for the week

The Lord be with you, — And also with you.
Let us pray to the Lord; *(silence, then the collect)* — Amen.

Free Prayer

General Collect

We give you thanks, God of love; you have guarded us through the night, and we pray you to protect us throughout this day, that all we do and our whole lives be full of your kindness, through Jesus Christ, your Son, our Lord,   — Amen.

The Lord's Prayer

O Christ, remember us in your Kingdom,
— Lord, teach us to pray: Our Father . . .

Blessing

Let us bless the Lord,
— We give our thanks to God.

May the peace of God, which surpasses all understanding, keep our hearts and our minds in Christ Jesus.
— Amen.

SATURDAY EVENING I

Introduction

Blessed be our God at all times,
now and always and for ever and ever.
— Amen.

Glory to you, our God! Glory to you!
Holy Spirit, Lord and Comforter,
Spirit of truth everywhere present,
filling all that exists,
Treasury of good gifts and Source of life,
come and dwell in us,
cleanse us from all sin
and in your love bring us to salvation:

— God, holy; God, strong and holy; God, holy and immortal;
have pity on us.

Psalm — Epistle

Responses

In the day of my distress I seek the Lord,
at night I hold out my hands.
— In the day of my distress . . .

I remember the great deeds of the Lord;
I remember former days and your wonders.
— At night I hold out my hands.

Glory to the Father, and the Son and the Holy Spirit.
— In the day of my distress . . .

Silence — Hymn

Intercession
May our evening prayer rise up to you:
— Lord, may your kindness descend upon us.

In faith let us pray to God our Father, his Son Jesus Christ and the Holy Spirit:
— O Lord, hear and have mercy (*or:* Kyrie eleison).

For the Church of the living God throughout the world let us ask for the riches of his grace:
— O Lord, hear and have mercy.

That our hearts and bodies be set free from all injustice, let us seek mercy of God:
— O Lord, hear and have mercy.

Grant peace to all who are now dying, and to those who sleep in Christ, O gracious Lord of Life:
— O Lord, hear and have mercy.

Grant us, Lord, to be fervent in believing and faithful in hope:
— O Lord, hear and have mercy.

Grant us, Lord, sincere obedience to your Word and truth in our love:
— O Lord, hear and have mercy.

Grant us, Lord, a life of thankfulness and peace:
— O Lord, hear and have mercy.

Grant us, Lord, the angel of peace and consolation, with the joy of all your saints:
— O Lord, hear and have mercy.

Collect for the week

The Lord be with you, — And also with you.
Let us pray to the Lord; *(silence, then the collect)* — Amen.

Free Prayer

General Collect

God of life, we give you thanks that you have revealed the light of our resurrection: as evening draws on we join to sing our hope, looking for the Coming of our Lord, Jesus Christ,
— Amen.

Blessing

Let us bless the Lord,
— We give our thanks to God.

May almighty God bless us,
the Father, the Son and the Holy Spirit.
— Amen.

Introduction to the Gospel

Psalm or hymn, *followed by a reading of the next day's Gospel or one of the Resurrection narratives.*

Song of Simeon

Now, Lord, give your servant his discharge,
— In peace, according to your promise.
For my eyes have seen your own Christ,
— Prepared by you for the nations.

A light to lighten all mankind,
— The glory of Israel your People.
Glory to Father, to Son and Holy Spirit
— For ever and ever. Amen.

SUNDAY MORNING II

Introduction

Praise the Lord, all nations, Alleluia.
— Celebrate his Name, all peoples, Alleluia.
Strong is his love for us, Alleluia.
— He is faithful for ever, Alleluia.

Psalm

Short Reading

I will give you a new heart, and put a new spirit in you. I will take out your heart of stone and give you a heart of flesh. I will put my Spirit in you; I will enable you to keep my laws, to observe my commands and to act upon them.

Song of Zechariah

Blessed be the Lord God . . . *(as on Saturday morning)*

Collect for the week

The Lord be with you, — And also with you.
Let us pray to the Lord . . .

SUNDAY EVENING II

Introduction

Blessed be our God at all times,
now and always and for ever and ever.
— Amen.

Glory to you, our God! Glory to you!
Holy Spirit, Lord and Comforter,
Spirit of truth everywhere present,
filling all that exists,
Treasury of good gifts and Source of life,
come and dwell in us,
cleanse us from all sin
and in your love bring us to salvation:
— God, holy; God, strong and holy; God, holy and immortal;
  have pity on us.

Psalm — Epistle

Song of Mary

Antiphon:
Sing and rejoice, O People of God,
for I have come to dwell among you.

My soul sings praises to the Lord,
my spirit glorifies my Saviour, my God!

For he has stooped to his humble servant,
and henceforth all ages will call me greatly blessed.
The Almighty chose me for his wonders;
Holy his Name!

And his love endures through the ages
to all who revere him;
he displays the strength of his arm,
and he scatters the conceited.

257

He will topple all the powerful from their thrones,
and raise up all the humble.
He feasts all the hungry with good cheer,
sends the rich away empty-handed.

He lifts up his own servant Israel,
ever remembering his love,
his ancient promise made to our fathers
in his oath to Abraham and to his race evermore.

Praise to Father, Son and Holy Spirit,
now and in the time to come
and for ever and ever.

Silence — Hymn

Intercession

Let my prayer rise before you like incense,
— And my hands like an evening offering.

————

Let us pray to the Lord with all our heart and all our mind:
— Have pity, Lord!

Lord almighty, God of our fathers, we implore you in your
great mercy, hear us and have pity on us:
— Have pity, Lord!

We pray for all Christians: may their lives be signs of joy and
of hope:
— Have pity, Lord!

We pray for bishops, and all who serve in your Church: may
our communion be a place of welcome, open to all humanity:
— Have pity, Lord!

We pray for all in authority: help them and direct them in
their decisions to establish justice and a society of sharing:
— Have pity, Lord!

We call to memory our fathers, mothers, our sisters and brothers now at rest in Christ; unite us, Lord, more and more in the joy of all your saints:
— Have pity, Lord!

We pray you, Lord, to keep us your servants in life, in peace and in health according to your kind will towards us:
— Have pity, Lord!

Collect for the week

The Lord be with you, — And also with you.
Let us pray to the Lord; *(silence, then the collect)* — Amen.

Free Prayer

General Collect

Lord, God almighty, come and dispel the darkness from our hearts, that in the radiance of your brightness we may know you, the only unfading light, glorious in all eternity, — Amen.

Blessing

Let us bless the Lord,
— We give our thanks to God.

May the Lord bless us, the Maker of heaven and earth.
— Amen.

MONDAY MORNING II

Introduction

Lord, open my lips,
— And my mouth shall proclaim your praise.
O God, come and help me,
-- Lord, support and save me.

God, you are my God, I seek you at sunrise;
— My soul is thirsting for you,
My body is pining for you,
— A parched land, weary and waterless;
I long to gaze on you in the sanctuary,
— To see your glory and power.

Better than life, your love,
— My lips will speak your praise;
All my life I would bless you,
— Lift up my hands at your name;
My soul feasting till satisfied,
— Joy on my lips, praise in my mouth.

Psalm — Old Testament

Responses

The Lord is with us, he is our stronghold!
+ God will help at the dawn of day.
— The Lord . . .

For us God is both refuge and strength,
there to help in time of need.
— God will help at the dawn of day.

We shall not fear, though the earth gives way,
and mountains tumble to the depths of the sea.
— God will help . . .

Come, consider the deeds of the Lord:
astounding, what he has done!
— God will help . . .

Be still and know that I am God,
exalted above the nations, exalted above the earth.
— God will help . . .

Glory to the Father, and the Son and the Holy Spirit.
— The Lord is with us . . .

Gospel — Silence

Intercession

Satisfy us with your love in the morning,
— And we will live this day in joy and praise.

———

Let us pray for the visible unity of Christians:
— Save us Lord; gather us from every nation.

Keep all who have found you, rooted in your love:
— May they grow in goodness and truth.

O Lord, remove our sins far from us:
— Deliver us for your name's sake.

God our defender, help us all:
— Look upon the face of your Christ.

Come soon, O Lord; how long?
— Have pity on your People's longing.

Show your work among your servants:
— May your glory shine for all mankind.

The gentleness of God be with us:
— Lord, continue what you have begun.

Collect for the week

The Lord be with you, — And also with you.
Let us pray to the Lord; *(silence, then the collect)* — Amen.

Free Prayer

General Collect

O Christ, our Lord; you are the way, the truth and the life: apart from you, we go astray, we cannot understand, and life without you is no life at all. Watch over our thoughts, our words and our actions, keep us throughout this day, so that all we do may be begun and completed in your name, blessed for ever and ever,   — Amen.

The Lord's Prayer

O Christ, remember us in your Kingdom,
— Lord, teach us to pray: Our Father . . .

Blessing

Let us bless the Lord,
— We give our thanks to God.

May the God of hope fill us with all joy and all peace in believing, that we may be overflowing with hope through the power of the Holy Spirit.
— Amen.

MONDAY EVENING II

Introduction

Lord, open my lips
— And my mouth shall proclaim your praise.
O God, come and help me,
— Lord, support and save me.

When I think of you as I sleep,
— Remember you through the night:
You have been my help,
— I rejoice in the shadow of your wings;
My soul leans upon you,
— Your right hand is holding me safe.

Psalm — Epistle

Responses

I will bless the Lord always and everywhere.
— I will bless . . .

His praises for ever on my lips.
— Always and everywhere!

Glory to the Father, and the Son and the Holy Spirit.
— I will bless . . .

Silence — Hymn

Intercession

Let my prayer rise before you like incense,
— And my hands like an evening offering.

————

We pray for all who confess the name of Christ. Keep faithful all who have consecrated their lives to your service, in the mutual love of marriage or in lives of celibacy for your Kingdom. Be their joy and their strength:
— Lord, hear us we pray.

For all in danger, those travelling far from home, in prison, in exile, victims of oppression: give them a joyful return:
— Lord, hear us we pray.

We pray for one another here: may we always be united in service and love:
— Lord, hear us we pray.

For all confronting trials and difficulties, who need kindness and mercy: give health to the sick and rest to those who are dying:
— Lord, hear us we pray.

We pray to be forgiven our sins, set free from all hardship, distress, danger, want, war and injustice:
— Lord, hear us we pray.

May we discover new ways of sharing the goods of the earth equitably amongst all peoples, struggling against exploitation, greed, or lack of concern: may all live by the abundance of your mercies and find their joy together:
— Lord, hear us we pray.

May we be strengthened by our communion with all Christ's saints:
— Lord, hear us we pray.

Collect for the week

The Lord be with you, — And also with you.
Let us pray to the Lord; *(silence, then the collect)* — Amen.

Free Prayer

General Collect

Lord God, we give you thanks for all your goodness to us today, for our bodies, hearts and minds: you watch over us and know what we need; may we accept both joys and troubles with a quiet faith and sure joy, through Jesus Christ, your Son, our Lord,   — Amen

Blessing

Let us bless the Lord,
— We give our thanks to God.

May the God of peace sanctify us wholly, keeping us blameless in body, mind and soul for the Coming of our Lord Jesus Christ.
— Amen.

TUESDAY MORNING II

Introduction

Lord, open my lips,
— And my mouth shall proclaim your praise.
O God, come and help me,
— Lord, support and save me.

Lord God, hear my prayer,
— Listen, God of Jacob.
God our shield, behold,
— Look upon the face of your Christ.

For me, a day in your courts
— Is better than a thousand elsewhere;
The doorway of the house of my God,
— Rather than a home with the wicked.

For God is bastion and armour,
— He gives us grace and glory.
The Lord refuses no good thing
— To all whose aims are true.

Lord, God almighty,
— Happy, who trusts in you!
How pleasant are your dwellings,
— God of all the worlds!

Psalm — Old Testament

Responses

I call to God and he hears me, by night, at dawn and
height of day,
+ His peace invades my soul, for he hears my cry.
— I call to God . . .

266

O God, hear my prayer,
give heed and answer me:
— His peace invades my soul, for he hears my cry.

Who will give me the wings of a dove,
that I may fly away and rest?
— His peace . . .

I long to flee far away,
and dwell in a desert place:
— His peace . . .

Cast all your burden on the Lord,
and he will support you:
— His peace . . .

Glory to the Father, and the Son and the Holy Spirit.
— I call to God and he hears me . . .

Gospel — Silence

Intercession

Satisfy us with your love in the morning,
— And we will live this day in joy and praise.

————

For the peace of the whole world and the salvation of all
mankind, let us pray to the Lord:
— Lord, have pity.

For justice in society, for the participation of all in political
decisions, for trust and friendship between all people — each
one created in the image of God and called to his Kingdom,
let us pray to the Lord:
— Lord, have pity.

For all who must struggle to earn their daily bread, for the unemployed and those unable to work because of sickness or discrimination; for the misfits on the edge of our society, and those living with them; for all who have no home, no family and no friends, let us pray to the Lord.
— Lord, have pity.

For the lonely, the abandoned and the deprived; for all who are despised and hopeless; for all who know nothing of the light of Christ and the Gospel, let us pray to the Lord:
— Lord, have pity.

Collect for the week

The Lord be with you, — And also with you.
Let us pray to the Lord; *(silence, then the collect)* — Amen.

Free Prayer

General Collect

O God our Father; your grace has been with us during the night, be with us now for the coming day: as you cause the sun to give warmth to the world, come and enlighten our hearts and minds by the brightness of your Spirit: may he lead us in ways of holiness, in communion with Christ who is love; your Son, our Lord,   — Amen.

The Lord's Prayer

O Christ, remember us in your Kingdom,
— Lord, teach us to pray: Our Father . . .

Blessing

Let us bless the Lord,
— We give our thanks to God.

May the Lord bless us and keep us; may Christ smile upon us and give us his grace; may he unveil his face to us and bring us his peace.
— Amen.

TUESDAY EVENING II

Introduction

Lord, open my lips,
— And my mouth shall proclaim your praise.
O God, come and help me,
— Lord, support and save me.

Praise, you servants of the Lord,
— Praise the name of the Lord!
Blessed be the name of the Lord,
— Blessed for ever and ever!
From the rising of the sun to its setting,
— Praised be the name of the Lord!

The Lord reigns over the nations,
— Exalted above the heavens, his glory!
Who can be compared to our God?
— He mounts towards his throne,
And descends to see heaven and earth.

He lifts up the weak from the dust,
— From the dunghill he raises the poor
To give them a seat with the princes,
— Yes, with the princes of his People;
He makes the childless woman
— The happy mother of children.

Psalm — Epistle

Responses

Ransom me, Lord, have mercy on me.
— Ransom me . . .

My feet follow the right path.
— Mercy on me.

Glory to the Father, and the Son and the Holy Spirit.
— Ransom me, Lord . . .

Silence — Hymn

Intercession

Let my prayer rise before you like incense,
— And my hands like an evening offering.

––––

Lord, we are sinners; grant us your pardon, and bring us to
true repentance:
— Lord, hear our prayer.

Guard and direct your Church in the ways of unity, service
and praise:
— Lord, hear our prayer.

Give to all nations true peace and a sense of the unity of
mankind:
— Lord, hear our prayer.

Make of our lives as Christians a place of communion and a
sign of resurrection in the world:
— Lord, hear our prayer.

Bring those without faith to the light of the Gospel:
— Lord, hear our prayer.

Confirm and keep us in your love, set in our hearts a longing
for your Kingdom:
— Lord, hear our prayer.

Give eternal life to all we have met today, our neighbours,
our friends, our enemies; preserve us from all destruction:
— Lord, hear our prayer.

Give us grace to share the fruits of the earth, until all mankind
enjoy the good things you have made:
— Lord, hear our prayer.

Grant a peaceful end and eternal rest to all who are dying, and your comfort to those who weep:
— Lord, hear our prayer.

Collect for the week

The Lord be with you, — And also with you.
Let us pray to the Lord; *(silence, then the collect)* — Amen.

Free Prayer

General Collect

Into your hands, Lord God our Father, we commit ourselves this night, body and soul and all that is ours. May your holy angels watch over us and the powers of darkness be dispersed, through Christ, our Lord,   — Amen.

Blessing

Let us bless the Lord,
— We give our thanks to God.

May the Lord of peace give us peace in all ways and at all times.
— Amen.

Introduction

Lord, open my lips,
— And my mouth shall proclaim your praise.
O God, come and help me,
— Lord, support and save me.

Come, shout for joy to the Lord,
— Sing to the Rock who saves;
With thanksgiving come before him,
— Praise him with music and song!

For the Lord is a great God,
— A great king above all gods,
In his hands are the depths of the earth,
— And the heights of mountains are his;
His the sea, for he made it,
— And the earth which his power has shaped.

Enter in, bend low, bow down;
— Let us kneel before God our Maker;
For he is our God and we
— The People whose shepherd he is,
The flock he leads with his hand.

Today if you hear his voice,
— Do not harden your hearts as at Discord,
That day of temptation in the desert,
When your fathers tested and proved me,
— Although they had witnessed my deeds.

Psalm — Old Testament

Responses

I will sing of your strength,
+ I long to praise your love every morning.
— I will sing . . .

Rescue me from my foes, my God,
protect me against my attackers:
— I long to praise your love every morning.

Yes, the Lord is my stronghold,
the God of my love comes to help me:
— I long to praise your love every morning.

You have been my stronghold,
a shelter in the day of anguish:
— I long to praise your love every morning.

I will make music for you, my Strength;
Yes, God is my stronghold,
he is the God I love:
— I long to praise your love every morning.

Glory to the Father, and the Son and the Holy Spirit.
— I will sing . . .

Gospel — Silence

Intercession

Satisfy us with your love in the morning,
— And we will live this day in joy and praise.

———

Remember, Lord, the People you have made your own from
the beginning:
— You ransomed them and made your home amongst them.

May happiness reign among them:
— And sadness be banished for ever.

Let us pray for all we shall meet today:
— Grant them eternal life.

Let us pray for those dying in Christ:
— Give them eternal rest, may light unfading shine for them.

Let us pray for our brothers far away:
— Save your servants who count on you.

Let us pray for all who are sad:
— Deliver them from their distress.

Let us pray for prisoners:
— Send them your help.

God of all creation, come and revive us:
— Smile upon us and we shall be saved.

Lord, hear our prayer:
— Let our crying be heard before you.

Collect for the week

The Lord be with you, — And also with you.
Let us pray to the Lord: *(silence, then the collect)*. — Amen.

Free Prayer

General Collect

Dear Lord, Creator of all; accept the prayers offered this morning by the Church of Christ; bring us all to your Kingdom, hallow and transform us by your grace, gather us into the unity of your love, through Christ, your Son our Lord, — Amen.

The Lord's Prayer

O Christ, remember us in your Kingdom,
— Lord, teach us to pray: Our Father . . .

Blessing

Let us bless the Lord,
— We give our thanks to God.

May the God of patience and of consolation grant us to live together after the pattern of our Lord Jesus Christ, so that with one heart and one voice we may give glory to God, the Father of our Lord Jesus Christ.

— Amen.

Introduction

Lord, open my lips,
— And my mouth shall proclaim your praise.
O God, come and help me,
— Lord, support and save me.

What joy when they said, "Let us go
    up to the House of the Lord"!
And now we have stayed our steps
    within your gates, Jerusalem.

Jerusalem! Built as a city
    which is one unified whole.
The tribes ascend to her gates,
    all the tribes of the Lord,

To celebrate the Name of the Lord,
    as is the custom in Israel,
In the place of the throne of justice
    and the house of David.

Pray for great days in Jerusalem:
    peace be on your tents!
May great days be seen in your walls,
    and peace in your dwellings!

In love for my brothers and my friends,
    I will say: Peace be on you!
In love for the House of the Lord
    I will pray for your happiness.

Psalm — Epistle

Responses

Great is our God, and great is his power!
— Great . . .

His wisdom knows no bounds,
— And great is his power!

Glory to the Father, and the Son and the Holy Spirit.
— Great is our God . . .

Silence — Hymn

Intercession

Let my prayer rise before you like incense,
— And my hands like an evening offering.

———

In faith let us pray to God our Father, his Son Jesus Christ
and the Holy Spirit:
— Lord have mercy and hear us. (*or:* Kyrie eleison).

For the Church of the living God throughout all the world, let
us ask the riches of his grace:
— Lord, have mercy and hear us.

For all who have begun to know Christ, and who long to
centre their lives on his will, let us beseech the kindness of
God:
— Lord, have mercy and hear us.

For all who are victims of weakness or wickedness, let us beg
the tender love of the Redeemer:
— Lord, have mercy and hear us.

For prisoners, for the defenceless who are exploited, for the
good who are persecuted, let us implore Jesus our Saviour:
— Lord, have mercy and hear us.

For the Christians in their divisions, for the Jewish people, for
those of whatever religion, for all unable to believe, let us
seek the Lord of truth:
— Lord, have mercy and hear us.

For all who serve their brothers and sisters, and strive for a nobler world and better lives for all, let us pray to the God of mercy:

— Lord, have mercy and hear us.

Collect for the week

The Lord be with you, — And also with you.
Let us pray to the Lord: *(silence, then the collect).* — Amen.

Free Prayer

General Collect

God of kindness and light; as the evening covers all things in darkness, cover and heal the sins we have committed this day: for so we shall find our peace in you, now and ever, — Amen.

Blessing

Let us bless the Lord,
— We give our thanks to God.

May our Lord Jesus Christ himself, and God our Father who has loved us, and given us by his grace eternal consolation and joyful hope, comfort our hearts and strengthen them in every good word and work.
— Amen.

THURSDAY MORNING II

Introduction

Lord, open my lips,
— And my mouth shall proclaim your praise.
O God, come and help me,
— Lord, support and save me.

Bring an offering and enter his House,
Worship God in the courts of his holiness,
— Fall before him, all the earth.

Go, tell the nations: God is king!
He made the worlds immovable.
— He will judge the nations justly.

Heavens, rejoice! And earth be glad!
— Let the sea roar, and all its creatures;
Let the earth rejoice and all its fruits,
— Let the forests shout for joy,

Before the Lord, for he is coming,
— He is coming to judge the earth;
He will judge the world with justice
— And the peoples with his truth.

Psalm — Old Testament

Responses

The love of the Lord is my song for ever,
+ From age to age my words proclaim your truth.
— The love . . .

I said: Your love will last for ever;
you have founded your truth in the heavens.
— From age to age my words proclaim your truth.

The heavens give thanks for your marvels,
your truth is proclaimed in the assembly of saints.
— From age to age . . .

Lord of all, who is like you?
Lord of power, robed in truth!
— From age to age . . .

Justice and judgement support your throne,
love and truth go before you.
— From age to age . . .

Glory to the Father, and the Son and the Holy Spirit.
— The love of the Lord . . .

Gospel — Silence

Intercession

Satisfy us with your love in the morning,
— And we will live this day in joy and praise.

———

We pray, Lord, for your Church in every corner of the world;
keep her faithful and renew her love until the end of time:
— Lord, hear our prayer.

We pray for all the ministers of the Church: bishops, priests,
and all set aside for your service: fill them with your Spirit
and make of them faithful bearers of your Word:
— Lord, hear our prayer.

We pray for all who lead the nations: may we enjoy days of
peace and play our full role in society:
— Lord, hear our prayer.

We give you thanks for all the believers who have enjoyed
your friendship from the earliest days: the patriarchs and
prophets, the apostles and martyrs, so many whose names you
know: may we too be counted among your faithful witnesses:
— Lord, hear our prayer.

280

We pray for our life together in your name; may the praise of Christ be overflowing in us all, by the grace of Jesus our hope:
— Lord, hear our prayer.

Collect for the week

The Lord be with you, — And also with you.
Let us pray to the Lord: *(silence, then the collect).* — Amen.

Free Prayer

General Collect

Lord our God, King of heaven and earth; sanctify today our hearts and our bodies, all that we undertake, and everyone we meet; may we live according to your will and bear the fruits of your Kingdom, through Jesus Christ, our Lord, — Amen.

The Lord's Prayer

O Christ, remember us in your Kingdom,
— Lord, teach us to pray: Our Father . . .

Blessing

Let us bless the Lord,
— We give our thanks to God.

May the God of peace enable us to do his will in every kind of goodness, working in us what pleases him, through Jesus Christ, to whom be the glory for ever and ever.
— Amen.

THURSDAY EVENING II

Introduction

Lord, open my lips,
— And my mouth shall proclaim your praise.
O God, come and help me,
— Lord, support and save me.

When the Lord brought back our prisoners,
    it seemed like a dream;
In our mouths there was laughter,
    on our lips there were songs.

In other lands they said: what marvels
    the Lord has done for them!
The Lord has done marvels for us,
    we were overjoyed!

Lord, bring home our prisoners
    like torrents in the desert.
The sowers who sowed in tears
    harvest with singing.

They went away weeping and sobbing,
    carrying the seed;
They come home laughing and singing,
    carrying their sheaves.

Psalm — Epistle

Responses

How varied are your works, O Lord!
— How varied . . .

All made wisely and well,
— O Lord!

Glory to the Father, and the Son and the Holy Spirit.
— How varied . . .

Silence — Hymn

Intercession

Let my prayer rise before you like incense,
— And my hands like an evening offering.

———

We pray, Lord, for this country and all who live here, the
poor, the immigrants, the old people and children, the victims
of society and of evil in our midst: save and defend them all.
— Lord, hear our prayer.

We pray for the peoples who are victims of our national
policies, and of the inequalities in the world: establish justice
by your power and let all nations share equally the good things
you have created for all mankind.
— Lord, hear our prayer.

We pray for the hungry and starving, the victims of constant
malnutrition: you are the bread of life, and call us to share
with those in need.
— Lord, hear our prayer.

We pray for those who hate and persecute our Christian
brothers and sisters on account of their faith and their service
of the poorest; be light and mercy for them, and give courage
to their victims.
— Lord, hear our prayer.

We pray for those newly converted and for those discovering
your love; strengthen us in faith and hope, deliver us in temptation, and forgive us all our sin.
— Lord, hear our prayer.

We pray for those far away, but dear to us; gather us again,
and bring us to the Kingdom of your Son, for you are the
Lord of all that live.
— Lord, hear our prayer.

Collect for the week

The Lord be with you, — And also with you.
Let us pray to the Lord: *(silence, then the collect).* — Amen.

Free Prayer

General Collect

Remain with us, O Lord, since the day is far spent and the night is coming; kindle our hearts on our way, that we may recognise you in the Scriptures and in the breaking of bread, for you live and reign for ever, — Amen.

Blessing

Let us bless the Lord,
— We give our thanks to God.

May the grace of our Lord Jesus Christ, the love of God and the communion of the Holy Spirit be with us all.
— Amen.

FRIDAY MORNING II

Introduction

Blessed be our God at all times,
now and always and for ever and ever:
— Amen.

Come, let us fall down and worship God our King:
— Come, let us fall down and worship Christ, our King and
our God.

Come, let us fall down and worship Christ among us, our
King and our God.
— God, holy; God, strong and holy; God, holy and immortal:
have pity on us.

Psalm — Old Testament

Responses

It is good to declare your truth through the night,
+ It is good to proclaim your love every morning.
— It is good to declare your truth ...

It is good to give thanks to the Lord,
to play for your name, God most high.
— It is good to proclaim your love every morning.

You have made me glad by your works, Lord,
seeing what you have done, I exclaim:
— It is good to proclaim your love every morning.

Lord, how great are your works,
and how deep your thoughts!
— It is good ...

The just will flourish like palm trees,
they will grow like cedars in Lebanon.
— It is good ...

Glory to the Father, and the Son and the Holy Spirit.
— It is good to declare your truth . . .

Gospel — Silence

Intercession

Christ loves us and has washed us from our sins by his blood:
— He has made us a People of priests for God our Father.

———

Have pity, Lord, we have sinned against you:
— Pardon, Lord, for all your People.

I confess my fault before you,
and I will hide my guilt no longer:
— Search and test me, Lord,
    try my heart and my desire.

In loving kindness answer,
in your tenderness regard me:
— Forget the wrongs of my youth,
    and remember me in your love.

Bring my soul out of prison,
that I may bless your name,
— Teach me to do your will,
    lead me by your Holy Spirit.

See, God comes to my aid,
together with all who support me:
— Master, you are pardon and goodness,
    full of love for all who call you.

Remember your kindness, O Lord,
and your love — they are for ever:
— You stretch out your hand and save me,
    your right hand does all that I need.

Collect for the week

The Lord be with you, — And also with you.
Let us pray to the Lord: *(silence, then the collect).* — Amen.

Free Prayer

General Collect

Lord Jesus Christ, Son of the living God; on the morning of your death you were brought before Pilate the Governor, and you, the Just, were condemned by the unjust; be full of mercy for us sinners when we stand before you on the last day, that we may reign with you in everlasting life,   — Amen.

The Lord's Prayer

O Christ, remember us in your Kingdom,
— Lord teach us to pray: Our Father . . .

Blessing

Let us bless the Lord,
— We give our thanks to God.

May God the Father, and our Lord Jesus Christ, grant us peace and love in believing.
— Amen.

FRIDAY EVENING II

Introduction

Blessed be our God at all times,
now and always and for ever and ever:
— Amen.

Come, let us fall down and worship God our King:
— Come, let us fall down and worship Christ, our King and
our God.

Come, let us fall down and worship Christ among us,
our King and our God.
— God, holy; God, strong and holy; God, holy and immortal:
have pity on us.

Psalm — Epistle

Responses

In your will is my song, I remember your name in the night.
— In your will . . .

Remember your promises, Lord.
— I remember your name in the night.

Glory to the Father, and the Son and the Holy Spirit.
— In your will is my song . . .

Silence — Hymn

Intercession

Christ loves us and has washed us from our sins by his blood:
— He has made us a People of priests for God our Father.

———

That his peace be shed in our hearts, and that we may remain
ever constant in believing, let us pray to the Lord:
— Have pity, Lord!

288

For peace in the world, and unity among Christians, that the Church may become a place of communion amongst men, let us pray to the Lord:
— Have pity, Lord!

For the Church of God, for all who gather in faith and prayer, let us pray to the Lord:
— Have pity, Lord!

For all the faithful, for their pastors and those who serve the charity of the Churches, let us pray to the Lord:
— Have pity, Lord!

That our work bring us nearer to God and earn us our daily bread, let us pray to the Lord:
— Have pity, Lord!

For the sick, the poor, the homeless and for all who suffer in body or spirit, let us pray to the Lord:
— Have pity, Lord!

Collect for the week

The Lord be with you, — And also with you.
Let us pray to the Lord: *(silence, then the collect).* — Amen.

Free Prayer

General Collect

Lord, we remember all who have died in faith until this very day; you give them rest in light, far from trouble and sadness, watching and shining over them; direct the ending of our lives in peace, and hasten the day when we shall all be gathered into the fulfilment of your perfect Kingdom, through Christ our Lord, — Amen.

Blessing

Let us bless the Lord,
— We give our thanks to God.

May the God of all grace, who has called us to his eternal glory in Christ, after we have suffered for a while, make us perfect, confirm and strengthen us; to him be the power for ever and ever.

— Amen.

SATURDAY MORNING II

Introduction

Lord, open my lips,
— And my mouth shall proclaim your praise.
O God, come and help me,
— Lord, support and save me.

I will sing and make music for you,
    awake now, my heart;
I will praise you among the peoples,
    and play for you among the nations.

High as the heavens, your love,
    your faithfulness as the clouds!
O God, arise in the heavens,
    your glory shine on the world!

Psalm — Old Testament

Song of Zechariah *(as Saturday Morning I)*

or: **Responses**

Lord, my hope is in you,
+ Bring me news of your love every morning.
— Lord, my hope . . .

Hear my prayer, O Lord,
hear me, for you are faithful and just.
— Bring me news . . .

I remember former times,
and think of all you have done.
— Bring me news . . .

I stretch out my hands towards you,
I am like dry, waterless ground.
— Bring me news . . .

Show me the way to walk in,
for I lift up my life to you.
— Bring me news . . .

Glory to the Father, and the Son and the Holy Spirit.
— Lord, my hope . . .

Gospel — Silence

Intercession

Satisfy us with your love in the morning,
— And we will live this day in joy and praise.

———

Protect, Lord, your People in every need:
— May love and sincerity reign in your Church.

Give your wise Spirit to all in power:
— Bless our cities and countrysides.

Show us how to share the fruits of the earth:
— Bless all who work for their living.

Comfort those in prison, defend and care for the old:
— Make an end of injustice in society.

Bless all peoples, and give us peace and harmony together:
— Show your mercy to all mankind.

Forgive our persecutors and slanderers, calm their hostility:
— Forgive our own injustices and correct them.

Lord, we remember all whom you have called to yourself:
— They have fallen asleep to rest in your presence.

Collect for the week

The Lord be with you, — And also with you.
Let us pray to the Lord: *(silence, then the collect).* — Amen.

Free Prayer

General Collect

O Lord, our sole refuge and our only hope; give us grace to consecrate ourselves tirelessly to your service in a great love for you and for our brothers, until that day when we come to the blessed vision of your face and you wipe away every tear from our eyes, in the Kingdom of Christ, our Lord, — Amen.

The Lord's Prayer

O Christ, remember us in your Kingdom,
— Lord, teach us to pray: Our Father . . .

Blessing

Let us bless the Lord,
— We give our thanks to God.

May the peace of God, which surpasses all understanding, keep our hearts and our minds in Christ Jesus.
— Amen.

SATURDAY EVENING II

Introduction

Blessed be our God at all times,
now and always and for ever and ever:
— Amen.

Glory to you, our God! Glory to you!
Holy Spirit, Lord and Comforter,
Spirit of truth everywhere present,
filling all that exists,
Treasury of good gifts and Source of life,
come and dwell in us,
cleanse us from all sin
and in your love bring us to salvation:

— God, holy; God, strong and holy; God, holy and immortal;
have pity on us.

Psalm — Epistle

Responses

Darkness with you is no darkness at all,
the night is clear as the day.
— Darkness with you . . .

If I were to say, Let darkness cover me,
let the night replace the day,
— The night is as clear as the day.

Glory to the Father, and the Son and the Holy Spirit.
— Darkness with you . . .

Silence — Hymn

Intercession

May our evening prayer rise up to you:
— Lord, may your kindness descend upon us.

Eternal God, by your Word you created all things visible and invisible: hear us, we pray.
— Have pity on us, Lord!

You govern the world and care for every person; hear us we pray:
— Have pity on us, Lord!

You created us in your goodness at the beginning of time and in its fulness you redeemed us for your glory; hear us we pray:
— Have pity on us, Lord!

In you are the ends of time, and you come to set us free; hear us, we pray:
— Have pity on us, Lord!

As we struggle to become your disciples, and to create justice in our world, hear us, we pray:
— Have pity on us, Lord!

For your People oppressed, suffering, sick, persecuted; hear us, we pray:
— Have pity on us, Lord!

Collect for the week

The Lord be with you, — And also with you.
Let us pray to the Lord: *(silence, then the collect).* — Amen.

Free Prayer

General Collect

Hear us, good Lord, as darkness is falling and grant us to find in you our rest; fill our hearts and our lives with such love that even our sleep becomes prayer and that we always be ready to welcome your Son when he comes in the glory of his Kingdom, bringing unutterable joy to all who wait for him; he is our Lord for ever and ever,   — Amen.

Blessing

Let us bless the Lord,
— We give our thanks to God.

May Almighty God bless us,
the Father, the Son and the Holy Spirit.
— Amen.

Introduction to the Gospel *(see: Saturday Evening 1)*

SUNDAY MORNING I

As on Sunday Morning II, with these, or other variants:

Short Reading

Blessing and glory, wisdom and thanksgiving, honour and power and strength to our God, for ever and ever!

Responses *(In place of the Song of Zechariah)*

You support me, so firmly I stand,
+ For ever you have set me before you.
— You support me . . .

Happy all who care for the poor and weak,
the Lord will care for them in their day of need:
— For ever you have set me before you.

God keeps me safe, he gives me life and happiness;
Lord, never let me fall into the Enemy's hands!
— For ever you have set me before you.

I said: Lord, have pity on me!
Heal my soul, for I have sinned against you:
— For ever you . . .

Raise me up, show me that you are my friend.
Blessed be your name, Lord God of Israel!
— For ever you . . .

Glory to the Father, and the Son and the Holy Spirit.
— You support me, so firmly . . .

SUNDAY EVENING I

As on Sunday Evening II, with these, or other variants:

Responses *(In place of the Song of Mary)*

In the beginning, the Word was;
The Word was with God and the Word was God.
— In the beginning ...

In the beginning, God created heaven and earth;
— The Word was with God and the Word was God.

Glory to the Father, and the Son and the Holy Spirit.
— In the beginning, the Word was;
The Word was with God and the Word was God.

Intercession

Let my prayer rise before you like incense,
— And my hands like an evening offering.

————

Let us pray for the men and women of every country:
— Have mercy, Lord!

For the unity of the Church and the salvation of all:
— Have mercy, Lord!

For all governments, and peace throughout the world:
— Have mercy, Lord!

For our families, our friends and companions at work:
— Have mercy, Lord!

For those who despise us, and for those who love us:
— Have mercy, Lord!

For all who need us to pray for them:
— Have mercy, Lord!

For all who are in danger as they travel:
— Have mercy, Lord!

For the liberation of all captives:
— Have mercy, Lord!

For all immobilised by sickness, and for the outcasts:
— Have mercy, Lord!

For all who are about to enter God's rest:
— Have mercy, Lord!

6 AUGUST: TRANSFIGURATION OF CHRIST

Introduction

Lord, how great is your love!
— In the shadow of your wings is our shelter.
In you is the source of life,
— By your light we see light.

You warm our hearts at the feasts in your house,
— You slake our thirst with waters of delight.
In you is the source of life,
— By your light we see light.

Keep in your love all those who have known you,
— In your goodness all who are upright.
In you is the source of life.
— By your light we see light.

Psalm (76, 83 or 103)

Old Testament (Ex. 24 9–18; 1 Kings 19 9–15a; or Dan. 7 9–10 and 13–14.)

Responses

Arise, shine, for your light has come!
— Arise . . .

And the Glory of the Lord has risen upon you.
— Your light has come!

Glory to the Father, and the Son and the Holy Spirit.
— Arise, shine . . .

Epistle (2 Peter 1 16–19)

Responses
Grace has now been revealed, our Saviour Jesus Christ has appeared.
— Grace . . .

The Lord has destroyed death; life and immortality shine
forth!
— Our Saviour Jesus Christ has appeared!

Glory to the Father, and the Son and the Holy Spirit.
— Grace . . .

Gospel (Matt. 17 1–9; Mark 9 1–10; or Luke 9 28–36)

Silence — Hymn

Intercession

You have crowned him with splendour and glory!
— You have set him over the work of your hands!

Loving Father, you transfigured your beloved Son and
revealed the Holy Spirit in the bright cloud: Enable us to
hear the Word of Christ with faithful hearts.
— Kyrie eleison.

You made light to rise in the darkness, and you have shone
in our hearts, to make known your glory in the face of Christ:
Revive in us the spirit of contemplation.
— Kyrie eleison.

You have called us by your grace, revealed in the appearing
of our Saviour Jesus Christ: Make life and immortality blaze
among us by your Gospel.
— Kyrie eleison.

You have given us your great love, and we are called your
children: When Christ is revealed, may we be like him, seeing
him as he is.
— Kyrie eleison.

O Christ, by your Transfiguration you revealed the Resurrection to your disciples before your Passion began; we pray for
the Church in all the difficulties of the world: In our trials, may
we be transfigured by the joy of your victory.
— Kyrie eleison.

301

O Christ, you took your friends with you and led them to a high mountain: May your Church stay close to you, in the peace and hope of your glory.
— Kyrie eleison.

O Christ, you led Peter, James and John down from the mountain and into the suffering world: When our hearts crave permanence, may we know the permanence of your love as you take us with you on your way.
— Kyrie eleison.

O Christ, you lightened the earth, when the Creator's glory rose upon you; we pray to you for all: May the nations come to your light.
— Kyrie eleison.

O Christ, you will transfigure our poor bodies and conform them to your glorious body; we pray to you for our brothers and sisters who are dying: That they may be changed into your likeness, from glory to glory.
— Kyrie eleison.

Collect

The Lord be with you, — And also with you.
Let us pray to the Lord: *(silence)*

O God, whose face we cannot see, you have made known your love by the lives of faithful witnesses. We give you thanks for the revelation of your glory in the face of our Lord Jesus Christ, for your confirmation of his disciples and for the promise of his victory. May the light of your presence shine in your People, that all may see the fulfilment of their hopes in the Coming of our Saviour, Jesus Christ, — Amen.

Free Prayer

302

Collect

Lord Jesus Christ, light shining in our darkness; have mercy on our tired and doubting hearts. Renew in us the courage we need, to bring to completion the work your calling has begun in us. Freely you gave your life on the Cross, freely you took it again in your Resurrection, you live and reign now, and for ever,   — Amen.

The Lord's Prayer

O Christ . . .

Blessing

Let us bless the Lord, alleluia!
— We give our thanks to God, alleluia!

May the Lord bless us and keep us; may Christ smile upon us and give us his grace; may he unveil his face to us and bring us his peace.
— Amen.

CELEBRATION OF CHRIST'S WITNESSES,
LITURGY OF SAINTS

Introduction

Rejoice in the Lord, you righteous!
— Sing for joy, all upright hearts!
Heaven, blaze in gladness,
— And all you saints, apostles, prophets!

Lord, I stand before you,
— You have taken my hand;
You will lead me by your counsel,
— And then bring me into glory.

Whom could I count on beside you?
— With you I desire nothing more on the earth.
My heart and my flesh are burned up,
— Rock of my heart, God, my portion for ever!

Coming to God is my wealth,
— I have taken the Lord for my refuge;
So I will tell all your works,
— At the gates of the daughter of Zion.

Psalm — Reading *(Old Testament or Epistle)*

Responses

(Apostles and witnesses)

The good never falter, They are remembered for ever.
— The good . . .

Happy are they who fear God,
and have great delight in his teaching.
— They are remembered for ever.

Their children will flourish and prosper,
the house of the upright is blessed.
— They are remembered . . .

He rises, the Light of the upright,
tender, compassionate and good.
— They are remembered . . .

Their justice remains for ever,
their heads are crowned with glory.
— They are remembered . . .

Glory to the Father, and the Son and the Holy Spirit.
— The good never falter . . .

(Saint John the Evangelist)
Their message covers the world, Good News to the ends of
the earth!
— Their message . . .

We have seen and we declare that the Father
has sent his Son to save the world.
— Good News to the ends of the earth!

Whoever shall confess that Jesus is God's Son,
God shall dwell in him and he in God.
— Good News . . .

God is love, whoever dwells in love
dwells in God and God in him.
— Good News . . .

God has given eternal life,
and this life is in his Son.
— Good News . . .

Glory to the Father, and the Son and the Holy Spirit.
— Their message . . .

(Saint Stephen)
Whoever looks to God will shine, No bitterness he shows.
— Whoever . . .

Stephen, full of grace and power,
performed wonders and signs among the people.
— No bitterness . . .

All eyes were on him,
his face was like an angel's:
— No bitterness . . .

He said: I see the heavens open,
and the Son of Man at God's right hand.
— No bitterness . . .

While they stoned him, he said:
Lord Jesus, receive my spirit,
Lord, do not charge them with this sin.
— No bitterness . . .

Glory to the Father, and the Son and the Holy Spirit.
— Whoever looks to God . . .

(Martyrs)

They will walk in the light of your presence;
They rejoice all day in your Name.
— They will walk . .

Lord, the heavens give thanks for your wonders,
for your truth in the communion of saints.
— They rejoice . . .

God, tremendous in the council of the saints,
God of all the worlds, who is like you?
— They rejoice . . .

You are the splendour of their power,
with your favour you crown them.
— They rejoice . . .

Glory to the Father, and the Son and the Holy Spirit.
— They will walk . . .

(Mary)
She believed the Lord would fulfil his Word,
all generations will call her blessed.
— She believed . . .

God has stooped over his humble servant.
— All generations . . .

Glory to the Father, and the Son and the Holy Spirit.
— She believed . . .

(All Saints and witnesses)
The righteous rejoice in the presence of God,
they exult and they dance for joy!
— The righteous . . .

To the Lord our God belong the secrets of life.
— They exult . . .

Glory to the Father, and the Son and the Holy Spirit.
— The righteous . . .

Gospel — Silence — Hymn

Intercession
Lord have mercy,
— Christ have mercy.

Lord have mercy,
— Christ hear us.

God the Father in heaven,
— Mercy for us!

God the Son, Redeemer of the world,
— Mercy for us!

God the Holy Spirit,
— Mercy for us!

God, one God, thrice holy,
— Mercy for us!

With the angels, the archangels and the spirits of the blessed,
Lord, we praise you!
— Glory! Lord of Life!

With the patriarchs and the prophets, Lord, we bless you!
— Glory! Lord of Life!

With the apostles and the evangelists, Lord, we give you
thanks!
— Glory! Lord of Life!

With all Christ's martyrs, Lord, we offer you our bodies in
sacrifice!
— Glory! Lord of Life!

With all the saints, witnesses to the Gospel, Lord, we consecrate our lives!
— Glory! Lord of Life!

With all the faithful of the Church, Lord, we adore you!
— Glory! Lord of Life!

Happy the dead who die in the Lord: now they shall rest from
their labours, for their works go with them.
— Glory! Lord of Life!

Collect

The Lord be with you . . .

Free Prayer

General Collect

(Apostles)

Father, of your infinite goodness, set us aflame with that fire of the Spirit Christ brought upon earth and longed to see ablaze, Christ who reigns with you and the Holy Spirit now and for ever,   — Amen.

(Marytrs)

Almighty God, there is no greater love than to give our lives for your friends. Grant us such courage, that in the company of your martyrs we may at last gaze with joy upon the face of Christ, and find in his glory the crown of your eternal life, — Amen.

(Mary)

God of all holiness, you manifested your love in such signs of grace, that Mary sang and rejoiced in your Spirit. Grant us such obedient hearts, that we like Mary may believe in your Word, and be gladdened by the gift of your Son, Jesus Christ, our Lord,   — Amen.

(All Saints)

Almighty God, break the power of darkness, let your glory appear among us and make us sharers of your eternity, with all your saints, through Jesus Christ, our Lord,   — Amen.

The Lord's Prayer

O Christ . . .

Blessing

Happy are you if they persecute you,
— If they slander you because of Christ.
Be glad and leap for joy,
— For your reward in heaven is great!

Let us bless the Lord,
— We give our thanks to God.

May grace be with all who love our Lord Jesus Christ in life incorruptible.
— Amen.

PRAYER AT THE MIDDLE OF THE DAY

No set form can be given for a moment which is necessarily caught up in the multiple tensions of a working day. A basic structure for this time might be:

Introduction

Psalm, Hymn or Song

Short Reading

Responses

Silence

Hymn or Song

Prayer

A number of elements of the morning or evening celebrations can also be used at midday, and these are gathered here:

From the depths I call to you, O Lord:
— Hear my cry!
Let your ear be attentive
— To the words of my prayer.

If you should retain our faults,
— Lord, who could stand?
But with you there is forgiveness:
— I worship and I hope.

My soul waits for the Lord,
— I am sure of his Word;
My soul relies on the Lord,
— More than a watchman on the dawn.

Since grace is found with the Lord,
— And the fullest of ransoms,
It is he who will ransom Israel
— From all his faults.

Hymn

Christ has risen from the dead,
the first fruits of those who fall asleep.
— Death is conquered by life.

Christ has risen from the dead,
death is swallowed up by Life.
— Where then, death, is your victory?

Christ has risen from the dead,
to the God of salvation let us give thanks evermore,
— Through our Lord Jesus Christ.

Hymn of Job

I know that my Redeemer is alive,
and that he will arise on earth at last;
when I awake, he will set me beside him,
and, in my flesh, I shall see God.
I will see him, he will take my part,
my eyes will look on no stranger.
My heart is fainting within me.

Song of Moses

O sing to the Lord! He has broken through in power and glory,
and risen from the dead, alleluia!
— O sing . . .

The Lord is my strength and him alone I praise;
my life he has restored.
— O sing . . .

You will lead us on up to the mountain,
to your holy dwelling, Lord our God,
where you live and reign evermore and evermore.
— O sing . . .

Song of Mary

Antiphon:

Sing and rejoice, O People of God,
for I have come to dwell among you.

My soul sings praises to the Lord,
my spirit glorifies my Saviour, my God!

For he has stooped to his humble servant,
and henceforth all ages will call me greatly blessed.
The Almighty chose me for his wonders;
Holy his Name!

And his love endures through the ages
to all who revere him;
he displays the strength of his arm,
and he scatters the conceited.

He will topple all the powerful from their thrones,
and raise up all the humble.
He feasts all the hungry with good cheer,
sends the rich away empty-handed.

He lifts up his own servant Israel,
ever remembering his love,
his ancient promise made to our fathers
in his oath to Abraham and to his race evermore.

Praise to Father, Son and Holy Spirit,
now and in the time to come
and for ever and ever.

Song of Simeon

Save us, Lord, when we are awake;
guard us, Lord, when we are asleep;
awake we will watch with Christ,
and asleep we will rest in peace.

Now, Lord, give your servant his discharge,
— In peace, according to your promise.
For my eyes have seen your own Christ,
— Prepared by you for the nations.

A light to lighten all mankind,
— The glory of Israel your People.
Glory to Father, to Son and Holy Spirit
— For ever and ever. Amen.

Save us, Lord . . .

Song of Zechariah

Antiphon:

Through the love in the heart of our God,
the Rising Sun has come to us.

Blessed be the Lord God of Israel,
coming to ransom his People;

Raising up saving power
in the house of his servant David,
as he said by the mouth of his prophets,
his saints in the times of old:

He sets us free from oppression,
free from the hands of our foes;
his bond of love with our fathers,
his covenant binding for ever;

His oath to our father Abraham,
assuring us, that liberated from fear,
delivered from all oppression,
we serve him in goodness and love,
before him, throughout our days.

And you, to be called his prophet,
will walk in the presence of God,
to prepare the ways he shall come,
announcing his People's salvation
with pardon for all their sins.

Through the love in the heart of our God,
the rising Sun will come to us,
shining on those in the dark
who lie in the shadow of death,
and guiding our steps into peace.

Hymn

Jesus Christ is Lord!
— To the glory of God the Father!

Jesus, by nature divine,
would not retain for himself
his rank as equal with God.

He poured out his glory in love,
becoming a humble slave,
and living the life of a man.

And human in every way,
he abased himself still more, obedient to death,
death on a cross.

So God has exalted him high,
and given to him the Name,
the greatest of all the names,

So that at Jesus' Name
every knee should bend low
in heaven, on earth, in the depths.

And every tongue proclaim:
Jesus Christ is Lord,
to the glory of God the Father!

Song of the Firstborn

He is the Image of the unseen God,
— The Firstborn of all creation.
For in him all things were made,
— In heaven and on the earth.

All was created through him and for him,
— He was before all things, and everything exists in him;
He is also the Head of his Body, the Church,
— He is the Beginning, the Firstborn from the dead.

God meant all his fulness to live in him,
— And reconciled through him all creation to himself,
Everything on earth and everything in the heavens,
— All gathered into peace by his death on the Cross.

Responses

Come, Holy Spirit,
From heaven shine forth with your glorious light!
— Come . . .

Come, Father of the poor; come generous Spirit;
Come, light of our hearts!
— From heaven . . .

Perfect Comforter! Wonderful Refreshment!
You make peace to dwell in our souls.
In our labour, you offer rest;
in temptation, strength;
and in our sadness, consolation.
— From heaven . . .

Most kindly, warming Light! Enter the inmost depth of our hearts, for we are faithful to you.
Without your presence, we have nothing worthy, nothing pure.
— From heaven . . .

Wash away our sin, send rain upon our dry ground, heal our wounded souls.
With warmth bend our rigidity, inflame our apathy,
and direct our wandering feet.
— From heaven . . .

On all who put their trust in you, and receive you in faith,
shower all your gifts.
Grant that they may grow in you, and persevere to the end;
give them lasting joy! Alleluia!
— Come, Holy Spirit . . .

Song of the Spirit

The Father will give you another Comforter,
— The Spirit of Truth, to be always with you.
The Holy Spirit will teach you everything,
— He will recall to you all I said, alleluia!

When the Spirit of Truth comes,
— He will lead you into all the truth;
For he will not speak by himself,
— But all that he hears, he will tell, alleluia!

Hymn

Come, Holy Spirit,
— Inflame our waiting hearts!
Burn us with your love,
— Renew us in your life.

Hymn

Send forth your Spirit, Lord,
— Renew the face of the earth.
Creator Spirit, come,
— Inflame our waiting hearts.
Your Spirit fills the world,
— And knows our every word.

Glory to God our Father,
— To Jesus Christ, the Son,
To you, O Holy Spirit,
— Now and for evermore.
You are, you were, you come,
— Eternal, living God!

317

The Beatitudes

Happy the poor in heart, the Kingdom of Heaven is theirs.
Happy the gentle, they will share in the Promised Land.
Happy all who weep, they will be comforted.
Happy are the hungry and thirsty for justice, they will be filled.
Happy the merciful, mercy will be theirs.
Happy the clear in heart, they will see God.
Happy the creators of peace, they will be called Sons of God.
Happy all who are persecuted for what is right, the Kingdom of Heaven is theirs.
Happy are you, if they persecute you, if they slander you because of Christ: be glad and leap for joy, for your reward in heaven is great!

Hymn

Remember Jesus Christ, risen from the dead.
He is our salvation, our everlasting glory.
If we die with him, we shall live with him;
if we persevere, we shall also reign with him.

If we deny him, he will deny us.
If we fail him, he will not fail us:
he cannot deny himself;
these words are sure.

Prayer

Bless us, Lord, now, in the middle of the day;
be with us and all who are dear to us,
and with everyone we meet.
Keep us in the spirit of the Beatitudes:
joyful, simple, merciful. — Amen.